BBC MUSIC GUIDES

MENDELSSOHN CHAMBER MUSIC

BBC MUSIC GUIDES

Mendelssohn Chamber Music

JOHN HORTON

UNIVERSITY OF WASHINGTON PRESS
SEATTLE

Contents

Music example no. 4 is reproduced by permission of G. Schirmer, New York and London, and no. 17 by Peters Edition, London, Frankfurt and New York.

First published 1972 by the British Broadcasting Corporation
Copyright © John Horton 1972
University of Washington Press edition first published 1972
Library of Congress Catalog Card Number 72-551
ISBN 0-295-95251-2
Printed in England

Introduction

One morning in the spring of 1821, Weber was walking through the streets of Berlin with his pupil Julius Benedict, when a boy of twelve ran up and introduced himself as Felix Mendelssohn-Bartholdy. Weber was due at a rehearsal, but Benedict was carried off to the Mendelssohn home and made to play excerpts from the newly completed *Der Freischütz*; in return the boy played from memory a number of Bach fugues and Cramer studies. Calling again at the house a few days later, Benedict caught Felix at work on what was to be his Opus 1:

I found him seated on a footstool, before a small table, writing with great earnestness some music. On my asking him what he was about, he replied, gravely, 'I am finishing my new Quartet for piano and stringed instruments'.

I could not resist my boyish curiosity to examine this composition [Benedict himself was only sixteen], and, looking over his shoulder, saw as beautiful a score as if it had been written by the most skilful copyist. It was his first Quartet in C minor.

Having been interrupted, Felix jumped up, went to the piano, and played all the music from *Der Freischütz* he had heard from Benedict a few days before, with appreciative comments.

Then forgetting quartets and Weber, down we went into the garden, he clearing high hedges with a leap, running, singing, and climbing up the trees like a squirrel – the very image of health and happiness.

The C minor Quartet, though amazingly precocious and well able to stand up to performance by serious adult artists today, is no miracle; we must keep that word in reserve for the Octet that followed four years later. But what Benedict was witnessing was not only the dawn of a brilliant and tragically brief career. It was also the continuation, by a twelve-year-old, of the great tradition of chamber music inherited from Haydn, Mozart, and Beethoven. So far as the history of chamber music in general is concerned, Mendelssohn is now recognised as the most significant figure between Schubert and Brahms. More specifically in the field of the string quartet, he may even be accounted the greatest master of the medium between Beethoven and Bartók.

We do not always realise how close the young Mendelssohn was to the Vienna composers, not only in spirit but also in time. His Opus 1 was written when both Beethoven and Schubert were still alive, with some of their finest music yet to be composed.

Beethoven had not then completed the *Missa Solennis* or the Ninth Symphony or any of the last-period string quartets. Schubert had not written *Die schöne Müllerin,* the B minor Symphony, or, with the exception of the Trout Quintet, any of the chamber music which have made him immortal in this field: the Octet, the String Quartets in A minor, G major, and D minor, the two Piano Trios, and the Quintet with two cellos. In Mendelssohn's boyhood, therefore, early and middle period Beethoven and any of Schubert's earlier works that might have come his way would be contemporary music, with Haydn and Mozart only a generation in the past.

On the other hand it must also be remembered that despite the splendid legacy of the Viennese masters, the string quartet as an autonomous, completely integrated and perfectly balanced ensemble had not wholly kept its stability during the early decades of the nineteenth century. Haydn, Mozart and Beethoven had drawn the line clearly enough between their chamber and symphonic styles, and as a rule expected them to be performed under different conditions and by properly constituted bodies of players. Yet the nonchalance of quite eminent professional executants of Mendelssohn's time in approaching Beethoven's masterpieces of quartet writing seems nothing less than barbarous. As there were still few quartet teams regularly rehearsing and playing together – the Schuppanzigh quartet was a notable exception – a work would not infrequently be brought before the public by an *ad hoc* ensemble, gathered together at the behest of the virtuoso violinist-leader to provide his 'accompaniment'. Spohr's autobiographical writings are full of examples of such improvisation. At a gathering of music-lovers in Magdeburg, in 1804, he played (*sic*) quartets by Haydn, Beethoven and Mozart, concluding with the E flat Quartet by Rode, and noted with satisfaction: 'Everything was well accompanied, so that I was able to give all my attention to my playing.' At Leipzig, he was 'invited to a number of quartet evenings where, having first rehearsed them with my accompanists, I played my favourites, the first six quartets of Beethoven.' He attempted the same works in Berlin with a group of players that included the cellist Bernhard Romberg; these musicians, however, seemed entirely ignorant of Beethoven's Op. 18, Romberg being moved to remark, 'But, my dear Spohr, how can you play such baroque stuff?' At Hamburg, Spohr entrusted a wealthy amateur with the responsibility for engaging three other players to make up a quartet, with the result that he found himself with three competent violinists but no violist or cellist. Nor was the quartet medium itself always respected. Rossini arranged Haydn and Mozart quartets for his student orchestra at Bologna, and Cherubini turned one of his own symphonies into a string quartet – the second of his six, in C – rewriting only the slow movement. With the larger chamber ensembles, the practice of admitting the double bass to replace a second cello helped to blur the distinction between chamber and orchestral textures; a fashion for this set in when Dragonetti deputised for an absent cellist in one of Onslow's quintets, and the English contrabassist Howell took part in one of Spohr's double quartets as late as 1846.

The ensemble of solo strings, far from being universally accepted as the ideal form of chamber music, was also threatened by the increasing popularity of the piano-centred ensemble, and particularly the piano trio and the piano quartet. The trio for piano, violin and cello originated to all intents and purposes with Haydn, was developed into a powerfully expressive medium by Beethoven and Schubert, and enjoyed a remarkable vogue among composers and players during the period we are discussing. Mendelssohn himself was to contribute two outstanding works to this genre. The quartet for piano, violin, viola and cello was virtually Mozart's invention, and had been relatively little exploited by the generation after him. Why Mendelssohn should have begun his published output with three examples is an interesting question, to which an answer will be suggested later. For the moment, it should be noted that just as the violin recitalist tended to regard the rest of the string quartet as his 'accompaniment', so the pianist of the trio or quartet of which he formed the centre looked upon the strings as *his* 'accompaniment' in what was in effect a miniature piano concerto. This attitude was in fact shared by Mendelssohn, and not only in the early piano quartets which are described on their title-pages as being '*pour le Pianoforte avec Accompagnement de Violon, Alto et Violoncelle*', but also in connection with the much later piano trios; when agreeing to 'play' the first of these, in D minor, at Ella's Musical Union in 1844, he stipulated that the violinist Ernst should, if possible, be engaged to 'accompany' him. The development of the modern grand piano, and the influence of the pianist-composers Schumann and Brahms, brought the partnership of keyboard and strings into a new and closer relationship, while giving these mixed ensembles a still greater ascendancy over the string quartet. It may be asked why Mendelssohn, a keyboard virtuoso if ever there was one, should not have been affected by this process, or even hastened it. The answer lies in his relationship to the Viennese classics, the nature of his early musical education, and his sensitivity to string idioms and sonorities.

Mendelssohn and the Techniques of String Playing

A first-hand working knowledge of the violin and its relatives had been almost obligatory as a part of the equipment of the pre-Romantic composer. Bach and Handel, Haydn and Mozart, Beethoven and Schubert all possessed it. Mendelssohn comes at the end of this tradition of double-handedness; a brilliant executant on the piano and organ, he also played the violin and the viola to a standard that gave him a deeper insight into the nature of the string quartet and allied ensembles than his keyboard-biased contemporaries and successors – Schumann, Liszt and Brahms – could ever attain. There is abundant testimony to his practical skill. Ferdinand Hiller remembered an occasion in Leipzig in 1839 when Mendelssohn shared with Kalliwoda the viola parts in one of Spohr's double quartets and in Mendelssohn's own Octet: 'He never touched a stringed instrument the whole year round, but if he wanted he could do it – as he could most other things.' Another of his partners in viola-playing was Niels Gade, who was to carry his admiration for the Octet so far as to attempt a work of his own for the same combination.

Mendelssohn's earliest chamber compositions were produced under workshop conditions, for members of the family and their professional and amateur friends who met, Sunday by Sunday, for informal but exacting rehearsals and concerts. String players seem to have been numerous and accomplished, particularly around the year 1823 when Mendelssohn wrote the series of string symphonies which represent a vital, though until recently almost disregarded, phase in his technical development. Now that modern editions, performances, and recordings of these attractive works have become available, they throw much light on the origins of the composer's mastery of form, texture, and above all idiomatic writing for strings. In particular, they show that the Octet was not the isolated marvel that it was once thought to be, but that it came as the richest flowering of a style that grew out of unique practical circumstances. Although the string symphonies must be classified as orchestral works, and are therefore outside the scope of this Guide, it is necessary to point out some of their features which have a bearing on the chamber music.

Several of the symphonies contain experiments in unusual groupings of the instruments. No. 9 in C, for example, uses a quintet lay-out in its first and third movements (two violins, two violas, and 'bassi'), while the middle movement has no fewer than four violin parts, together with viola and 'bassi', and a *minore* section for two violas and 'bassi'. Incidentally, the third movement of this work, inscribed *Scherzo*, must be one of Mendelssohn's first essays in writing for strings in that characteristic style. The Symphony in D (No. 8), of which a version also exists with wind parts, has an *adagio* movement for three violas and 'bassi'. This predilection for the lower strings leads one to wonder if the curious *maggiore* section in the scherzo of the C minor Piano Quartet, Op. 1, laid out for viola, cello and the pianist's left hand only, may have been originally conceived as some form of string ensemble. Interesting also from this aspect is the Sextet of 1824, Op. 110, with its low-register scoring for one violin, two violas, cello, double bass, and piano. The finale of No. 11 in F (dated 12 July 1823) foreshadows the Octet in its mingling of passage-work, sustained harmonies and imitative entries.

The symphonies are no less interesting for their variety of structure. Some have three movements, some four, some only one. There may be a slow introduction, followed by a movement in sonata form. Fugal texture may be admitted into a sonata movement, as in No. 9 in C, or an entire first movement may be expressly described as *Fuga,* as in No. 12 in G. This willingness to make structural experiments, and especially to incorporate fugal elements into sonata forms, remains typical of Mendelssohn's chamber-music writing at its most vigorous and inventive, as in the String Quartets in A, Op. 13, and E flat, Op. 44, no. 3.

Following closely on the invaluable experience of writing the string symphonies, the influence of two notable violinists can be detected in the leap forward which Mendelssohn made in his quartet technique from the year 1824. It was in that year that he began to take lessons from Eduard Rietz, who was to die of consumption at the age of thirty; Mendelssohn admired him above all other violinists, and not only dedicated to him the Octet and the F minor Sonata for violin and piano, but also composed the intermezzo of the revised Op. 18 Quintet in his memory. Less close in personal friendship, but with more to offer in breadth of professional experience, was the Frenchman, Baillot, whom Mendelssohn met during his stay in Paris in 1825. Baillot was the doyen of the flourishing French school of violin playing, a fine technician who took chamber-music performance more seriously than any of his compatriots. He was one of the first quartet leaders to give public recitals of the earlier quartets of Beethoven and private performances of the later ones, and he was also known for his encouragement of young composers of advanced ideas. It was through his advocacy that Mendelssohn's String Quartet in A, Op. 13 – perhaps the most vital and certainly the most original of all his chamber works – was taken up with such enthusiasm by the Parisian string players in the 1830s. 'Is it not splendid,' Mendelssohn wrote home early in 1832, 'that my quartets should be played in the classes of the Conservatoire, and that the pupils there are practising their fingers off to play "Ist es wahr"~?' (see p.30). It may have been Baillot also who introduced Mendelssohn to the E flat String Quartet of Cherubini, a work – written in 1809 – that he came to know through playing the viola in it, and whose scherzo-trio anticipates the type of airy movement which is often thought of as originating with Mendelssohn:

Ex. 1

Allegretto moderato

Tradition and Development in Mendelssohn's Chamber Music

Towards the end of his life, Mendelssohn told his Leipzig students that his own teacher, Zelter, used to require him to compose on the model of a Haydn quartet, imitating the form exactly, and he commended to them this method of study. It was just as well that Zelter should have encouraged his pupil to learn from Haydn, who always carried his erudition so lightly and, in the Op. 20 Quartets, showed how fugal procedures could be integrated with instrumental sonata forms. Zelter's own contrapuntal disciplines were imposed with a heavier hand, as we can see from the quartet fugues Mendelssohn was made to write: an example survives as the finale of the E flat Quartet of 1823, and perhaps another as the isolated fugue, also in E flat, in Op. 81. The influence of Haydn can be traced not only in the formation of an elegant linear style, with complete freedom for the four instruments to vary their spacing and to cross one another for some particular effect of colour, but also in the imitation of such procedures as the derivation of second-subject material from the principal theme and the arrangement of new and surprising series of events in the recapitulation of sonata movements. In addition, his study of Haydn's quartets must have strengthened his naturally firm sense of key-balance and of modulatory effect.

After Haydn, the strongest influence is that of Beethoven, becoming apparent almost to the point of direct quotation in the Quartets Op. 12 and Op. 13. Mendelssohn was evidently ahead of his time in grasping the importance of the whole range of Beethoven's chamber music, from the Op. 18 Quartets which Spohr found so little known outside Germany, to the last-period works which were still being written during Mendelssohn's boyhood. Beethoven's cyclic and integrating experiments held a special fascination for him, as can be seen from the two early quartets just referred to. It is thought that one of Mendelssohn's piano teachers, Ludwig Berger, may have encouraged him to think along these lines, paying special attention to motival construction and the transference of thematic ideas from one part of a work to another. It is an interest that seems to fade out in Mendelssohn's later works; there is only a slight trace of it in what is perhaps the most Beethovenish of his Quartets, the F minor, Op. 80.

The total output of Mendelssohn's chamber music is not large; it amounts to no more than six completed string quartets with opus numbers, the Octet for strings, two string quintets, two piano trios, a handful of works of duo sonata type, and the three early piano quartets and the Piano Sextet. Both for this reason, and because of the fact that no clearly marked development or change took place, technically or stylistically, as his remarkable adolescence passed into mature manhood, it would be meaningless to attempt a conventional 'period' classification. It is relevant, however, to note that Mendelssohn started his composing career with chamber music and was for ever longing to return to it. We may therefore distinguish points in his life at which this medium occupied an especially prominent place in his creative interests and activity.

One such phase is indicated in a letter to Hiller, dated 17 August 1838, in which Mendelssohn writes:

A very important branch of pianoforte music, which I am particularly fond of — trios, quartets, and other things with accompaniment (*sic*) — is quite forgotten now, and I feel greatly the want of something new in that line. I should like to do a little towards this. It was with this in mind that I lately wrote the Sonata for violin, and the one for cello, and I am thinking next of writing a couple of trios.

The violin sonata he refers to is probably the one in F major, which suffered an unmerited eclipse until Yehudi Menuhin rediscovered and published it. The Cello Sonata must be the first, in B flat; it was written in 1838, and the Piano Trio in D minor belongs to the following year. Mendelssohn thus announces his intention of turning aside, if only temporarily, from the pure string chamber music of the period 1825 to 1838 – that is, from the Octet to the three String Quartets of Op. 44 – and exploring anew the field of concerted works with piano; his expression 'with accompaniment' shows that he still followed the fashion of regarding the keyboard instrument as the basis of the ensemble and the strings as ancillary. As a matter of fact, we are so used to thinking of Mendelssohn as the composer of numerous, and often slight, piano pieces that we forget that during the first half of his life he preferred to write for the keyboard 'with accompaniment'; thus when the publisher Nägeli asked him in or about 1826 for some solo piano pieces he replied that he had none to offer, adding: 'Sonatas with violin or tenor, quartets, etc., have always had more attraction for me.'

After the composition of the first Piano Trio, in 1839, Mendelssohn's interest in chamber music appears to recede once again, or more probably his increasing responsibilities as performer, conductor, and administrator restrict his creative output as a whole. Curiously enough, the gap is filled as it were by proxy, the year 1842 being Schumann's *annus mirabilis* of chamber music, with the completion of the three string quartets (dedicated to Mendelssohn), the Piano Quintet, and the Piano Quartet. Perhaps it was the dedication of this last work to the cello-loving Count Mateusz Wielhorski that brought Mendelssohn himself back to the chamber-music fold, with a Sonata (Op. 58, written in 1843) for the same distinguished amateur. This was followed by a revival of pure string writing. Some of the products of this phase are included in the posthumous miscellany published as Op. 81: a Capriccio in E minor, in the form of an introduction and fugue, written in 1843, and an *andante* and scherzo from 1847, the last year of his life, which were probably intended to form part of a String Quartet in E. To these must be added the second String Quintet, Op. 87, and the composer's final legacy to the quartet repertory – the powerful work in F minor, Op. 80, finished in the summer of 1847, when he had begun to recover some of his vitality after the shock of his elder sister's sudden death.

If Felix himself had been granted more years, he would almost certainly have insisted on setting aside more time for composing, and especially for writing chamber music. He told the English critic, Henry Chorley, earlier in the same year that he intended to withdraw himself from public life, from the incessant travelling, conducting, playing, and administration that were wearing him out and continually interrupting his creative work. He would make his home somewhere in the Rhineland where, he promised Chorley, 'I shall be near England, and can come over as often as you wish; and I shall be within reach of our towns with all these new railroads; but I must live quietly, and get rid of all that noise and interruption, if I *am* to live.'

The profundity of feeling in the F minor Quartet suggests very strongly that in returning to chamber music Mendelssohn might have found not only the spiritual restoration he longed for, but also a cleansing of the mind from the effects of years of over-production of large-scale works, mostly depending on broad choral effects and rhythmically constrained by verbal metres, which had undeniably brought about a certain coarsening of style. His instinct was right when he said that music in itself was a mode of expression more exact and pregnant than any words could ever be. It was only in his instrumental works, and above all in the best of his chamber music, that his imagination could take to its wings, and these are the compositions on which his future reputation will almost certainly depend.

The Early Concerted Chamber Music with Piano: the Piano Quartets and the Sextet

Although these compositions must always appear as apprentice work beside the radiant mastery of the series of string quartets that was soon to follow them, they are too good to be overlooked altogether, and it is satisfying to observe them stealing back into the professional repertory. The composer – or his elders – after all thought so well of them as to make them his earliest publications, and they rapidly won the admiration of influential patrons and artists. The B minor Quartet in particular attracted the attention of Baillot and other leading French musicians; Cherubini gave it gracious if qualified praise ('Ce garçon est riche; il fera bien; il fait même déjà bien, mais il dépense trop d'argent, il met trop d'étoffe à son habit'); and Goethe allowed it to be dedicated to him. All three quartets are abundant in the sound and tasteful craftsmanship Mendelssohn achieved so early and apparently with little effort, in the imaginative fertility that finds its fullest expression in the various types of middle movement occurring in these works, and in a bold attitude to form and harmony which is sometimes lacking in his later career.

The C minor Piano Quartet, Op. 1, had been begun during a holiday in Switzerland early in 1821. The score on which Julius Benedict watched the young composer at work may well have been the fair copy, now in the British Museum. Its faultless calligraphy, with the elegant dedication to '*Son Altesse Monseigneur le Prince Antoine Radziwill*', fully deserves Benedict's wonder and praise. Prince Radziwill was a frequent guest at the Sunday-morning concerts, and must have been highly respected, not so much for his rank as for his friendship with Beethoven and his own ability as a composer. Did he recall that Beethoven, at the age of fourteen, had written *Trois quatuors pour clavecin, violino, viola e basso* (though these remained unpublished until after his death), and suggest to the Mendelssohns that a talented boy could not do better than follow such a precedent? If so, he could hardly have imagined how far the young Mendelssohn would surpass the young Beethoven in his handling of the instruments.

The evidences of extraordinary talent appear in the very first bars, where each of the bowed instruments enters with its own sharply characterised motive, to combine with its fellows in the most natural way. Keyboard and strings are treated with equal assurance, idiomatically and with a sensitive balance of interest. But what arouses one's strongest admiration is the absolute control of large-scale structure, the confident organisation of modulations, and as rich a harmonic resourcefulness as the composer was to show at any time of his life. In the A flat *adagio* the depth of feeling is enhanced by the sombre colours of viola and cello and by the sonorous ensemble provided by the strings as background to some delicate keyboard figuration. Reference has already been made to the third movement, one of the Mendelssohnian scherzo-types, and to its oddly-scored *maggiore*. The finale uses the same material for first and second subject themes, a measure of economy that gives little ground for Cherubini's charge of prodigality.

The F minor Piano Quartet, Op. 2, was finished on 3 December 1823, and dedicated to '*Monsieur le Professeur Zelter par son élève Felix Mendelssohn-Bartholdy*'. It hardly comes up to the standards of its companions in structural mastery, but is of considerable interest through its explorations of a key to which the composer was to return for his last completed string quartet. For the *adagio* he goes to the submediant key of D flat and modulates adventurously; the strings bring this movement to an end with a barely audible cloud of vibrant harmonies. The intermezzo is an example of one of the alternatives Mendelssohn sometimes chose in place of the more elaborately developed scherzo; this is a brief, simple movement without a trio, and in the tonic key of F minor. The finale, *allegro molto vivace,* is a brilliant if rather prolix movement, with piano figuration in the manner of Weber, who was very much Felix's hero at this time.

The B minor Piano Quartet, Op. 3, was completed on 18 January 1825. It is by far the finest and most mature of the three, and indeed has claims to be ranked among the best of the composer's instrumental music. It is also the first work in which he attempts to carry out systematically the ideas of theme transformation, from movement to movement, which he is believed to have learnt from Berger; the initial theme of the first movement reappears in another shape in the scherzo, and again in other forms in the finale. The Quartet opens, like its fellows, with a bold assertion from the piano:

Ex. 2

Allegro molto

The composer recognised this as daring, if not revolutionary, jokingly associating it a few years later with the St Simonist movement that kept the Paris police busy at the time of his visit there in 1832. This motive drives the *allegro molto* with great energy and integrates it throughout, though there are also strong secondary themes, and an important new idea is introduced as late as the development section – hence, perhaps, Cherubini's remark. Mendelssohn was later to regard the *andante* (in E major) as conventional and over-sweetened; but if the influence of Spohr can be detected in its chromatic lyricism, it must be conceded that there is also Spohr-like acuteness for instrumental sonorities and ability to clarify complex textures. The third movement is a superb Mendelssohn scherzo, marvellously written but demanding much of the performers: it might well become a popular light movement on its own, or a standard encore piece if piano quartets were addicted to such frivolities. The key is F sharp minor, with a middle section in B major. Humorous and brilliant though the finale is (*allegro vivace*), and full of ingenious contrapuntal witticisms, it has to work hard to cap the scherzo. The last few bars, however, round off the whole work in a striking fashion, with rhythmical transformations of the semitonal theme heard in the opening bars (Ex. 2):

Ex. 3

No account of the B minor Piano Quartet would be complete without Mendelssohn's lively description of what happened when Baillot and his colleagues read it for the first time, presumably with the composer at the piano:

Baillot was rather confused at the beginning, and played even carelessly, but at one passage in the first part of the first movement he caught fire, and played the rest of the movement and the whole *adagio* very well and with much vigour. Then came the scherzo; and he must have liked the beginning, for now he began to play and hurry in earnest, the others after him, and I trying in vain to stop them. But who can stop three runaway Frenchmen? And so they took me with them, madder and madder, and faster and louder. Baillot especially, at a place near the end, where the theme of the trio is taken up against the beat, played fearfully loud; and as it had happened to him to make a mistake several times before, he got into a perfect rage with himself. When he had finished, he said nothing but 'Encore une fois ce morceau'. Now everything went on smoothly, but wilder even than before. In the place quite near the end, where the theme in B minor comes in once more fortissimo, Baillot produced a hurricane in the strings that put me in fright of my own quartet. And as soon as it was finished, he came up to me again without saying a word, and embraced me twice, as if he wanted to crush me.

Although the Sextet in D major has been in print since Novello published it among the posthumous works as Op. 110, it has been the most neglected of all the chamber music. Its unusual scoring, for one violin, two violas, cello, double bass and piano, is doubtless part of the reason for this, but it must also be admitted that it is less even in quality than the piano quartets. There are, however, signs of growing interest among artists and the public: a miniature score is now available, and the work has been recorded by members of the Vienna Octet.

The Sextet was written about the same time as the B minor Quartet – the end of the piano part bears the date 10 May 1824, just two months after Schubert had finished his Octet for wind and strings. In the first movement, Mendelssohn uses the string group mainly as an unobtrusive and technically undemanding background to a virtuoso piano part which recalls, like much of the keyboard writing in the piano quartets, the style of Weber. The following *adagio,* in the mediant key of F sharp major, holds greater musical interest, being concisely but poetically written, with effective dialogue between muted strings and keyboard. The third movement, though quaintly described as 'Menuetto', is a tense, compact 6/8 scherzo in D minor (again Schubert comes to mind, for he must have been writing his 'Death and the Maiden'

Quartet at this very time). This movement has a central trio section in F major, where chromatic piano scales flash across more demure string phrases. For his finale Mendelssohn has recourse to the contemporary fashionable bravura rhythms of the galop, in the bright key of D major; yet not all is superficial glitter, the secondary material especially revealing Mendelssohn's growing admiration for Bach; at such moments the string group divides into five real parts, with independent movement between cello and bass. But the most original stroke is kept until near the end, when after reaching a powerfully rhetorical climax the whole ensemble plunges into a recall of the D minor scherzo, developed more elaborately than in its original position as the 'Menuetto'. The galop motive returns in the coda, but remains in the stormy key of D minor almost to the last, the major tonic chord being reached only in the final cadence. Once again Mendelssohn is trying out cyclic procedures, as in the third Piano Quartet; he was soon to make even more telling use of them in the Octet for strings and in the String Quartet in A.

Early Sonatas for Solo Instruments and Piano

W. S. Newman states, in *The Sonata since Beethoven*,[1] that 'Mendelssohn wrote about half of his sonatas, including all those for piano, in the six years from age twelve to eighteen.' The first Piano Sonata, in G minor, in fact preceded the piano quartets in order of composition, though it was published, as Op. 105, only after Mendelssohn's death. Some of the earlier duo sonatas must now be discussed very briefly, leaving later and more mature works of a similar kind for a subsequent section.

Of this group, only the Sonata in F minor for violin and piano, Op. 4, was published in the composer's lifetime. It was written in 1823, when he was fourteen, and was dedicated to Eduard Rietz. It is a derivative work, owing much to Mozart and Beethoven, but quite worthy of attention in its own right, with plenty of interest for both performers. The young composer's command of contrapuntal resource is strongly in evidence, and also his remarkable skill in modulation. The work is romantically coloured. It begins with an unaccompanied recitative for the violin; the second

[1] University of North Carolina Press and Oxford University Press (1969).

movement (*poco adagio*) starts sedately, like a slow minuet, but soon becomes rhapsodical, with careful directions for the use of the second, third and fourth strings of the violin; and the last movement (*allegro agitato*) culminates in another cadenza leading to a coda whose rather vapid brilliance is redeemed by the graceful sentiment of the final pianissimo cadence. After its use in this early Sonata, the tragic key of F minor was to be absent from the chamber music until nearly twenty years later, when it returned in the composer's last and possibly greatest string quartet.

A sonata for Mendelssohn's favourite instrument, the viola or 'tenor', with piano had long been known to exist, but has only recently been published from the autograph in the Berlin Staatsbibliothek. It was composed between 23 November 1823 and 14 February 1824. This combination of instruments in a large-scale work clearly set Felix problems that even his precocious talent was not yet equal to. Not only are there vacillations of style, but there are also not a few crudities of a kind we hardly expect in a composition of Mendelssohn at any age; most of them arise from that well-known trap for the elementary student, the attempt to complete ambiguous progressions in a keyboard part by supplying essential notes from a voice or instrument of different colour. This and other technical difficulties were to be solved some fifteen years later in the first Cello Sonata, for which the Viola Sonata might be considered a preliminary study. Both works look back to Beethoven's glorious A major Cello Sonata, Op. 69. The Viola Sonata has an *adagio* introduction followed by three main movements, all alike in the key of C minor with only the slight relief of a change of mode for the minuet-trio. In the first movement the viola is freely used over its compass, though there is a tendency to starve the telling low register of melodic interest and assign to it mostly pedal notes and other harmonic elements, while the piano part, as already noted, sometimes sacrifices completeness and logic in its anxiety to avoid submerging the viola. The minuet contains some of the best writing, being evidently modelled on the scherzo of Beethoven's Op. 69, but it falls down badly in the trio, a naive little chorale in C major (of which, however, some use might be made as a teaching piece for beginner violists). The most curious feature of the Sonata is its enormous finale, a set of variations on a theme closely resembling that of the *Variations sérieuses* for piano, Op. 54. In the variations themselves the piano part becomes progressively, if not altogether intelligibly, elaborate, perhaps in vain emulation of Beethoven's variation-movement in the Kreutzer Sonata, though Mendelssohn's viola, unlike Beethoven's violin, is given an ever-diminishing share in the proceedings.

Of much greater importance is the E flat Sonata for clarinet and piano, which also remained unpublished and unknown until 1941; it was later edited by Eric Simon in a collection of *Master works for clarinet and piano* published by Schirmer. This edition claims to be based on the composer's autograph 'at present in a private collection in the United States'. The Sonata seems to have been composed about 1825, probably for Heinrich (Joseph) Bärmann, a member of the Munich Court Orchestra and a close friend of Mendelssohn, who frequently corresponded with him. His two sons, Carl and Heinrich, were also clarinettists, and during a visit to Munich in October 1831 the family performed an arrangement of Beethoven's String Quartet in F, Op. 18, no. 1, for two clarinets, corno di bassetto, and bassoon. Mendelssohn had a hand in this arrangement, which probably gave him the idea for the *Concertstücke* written in the next year. It was not the first time that the elder Bärmann had inspired original works for his instrument: some ten years earlier Weber had dedicated to him his Clarinet Quintet and the Grand Duo Concertante for clarinet and piano.

On the evidence of Simon's edition, Mendelssohn's Clarinet Sonata is a valuable addition to the repertory of the instrument, conceived with much insight into its capabilities and full of melodic and contrapuntal interest. It starts with an introductory *adagio* in the style of a song without words and ending on the dominant with a clarinet cadenza. Then follows a lengthy *allegro moderato* (the editor suggests cuts), among whose attractive features may be mentioned the elegant second-subject themes reminiscent of Weber, the bell-like passage occurring first at the close of the exposition, and most of all the finely organised development, terse and virile, which reaches a climax with bold dissonances over a dominant pedal before the return of the principal theme. The *andante* (in G minor – all the other movements being in E flat) is again a song without words, of a highly distinctive character; nowhere did Mendelssohn write a melody of greater charm than the one announced here, by the clarinet without accompaniment, and later harmonised and extended:

Ex. 4 Andante

The finale is a light-hearted movement, with a vein of wit that would not have discredited Haydn or early Beethoven. The development section of this movement produces, in imitative passages, a harmonic piquancy that may surprise those who persist in exaggerating the limitations of Mendelssohn's idiom.

The two *Concertstücke* for clarinet in B flat and basset horn in F with piano accompaniments were written, as already noted, in 1832 for two of the foremost virtuosi in Europe and published as Op. 113 and 114. The F minor work begins with an *allegro con fuoco* which is well designed to display both the tonal range of the instruments and their capacity for lyrical expression. In this movement most of the melodic interest is given to the clarinet, while the basset horn demonstrates its effectiveness in accompanying arpeggio figures. Cadenza-like passages lead to the *andante,* in A flat major. Here the two wind instruments discourse in the manner of an operatic duet, with much use of thirds and sixths, against a piano background of broken chords. The final *presto* starts in F minor but the mode soon changes to major and the rhythm to a brisk 6/8, like that of the *Rondo capriccioso* for piano. Again there is a profusion of runs and arpeggios for the wind instruments.

The other *Concertstück,* in D minor, follows a similar pattern. The first movement (*presto*), is succeeded by a romance in 6/8 time (*andante*), in the key of F major. The finale, marked *allegretto grazioso,* is in the style of a galop, with brilliant display writing making use of dialogue between the instruments, passages in rapid thirds, and the wide-ranging arpeggios so congenial to the clarinet family. Though of limited musical importance, these two pieces deserve to be explored by woodwind specialists in search of material for technical study and concert performance.

The Octet in E flat, Op. 20[1]

This magnificent work, as we have seen, need no longer be viewed as an isolated phenomenon, but may be regarded as the finest flowering of the young Mendelssohn's absorbing interest in the almost infinite possibilities of dividing and grouping a full ensemble of strings. Far from diminishing his achievement, this realisation enhances its wonder. The string orchestra almost passed out of existence as an independent unity between the decline of the *concerto grosso* in the middle of the eighteenth century and its resurgence with the later romantics – Dvořák, Tchaikovsky, Grieg and the rest – and its eventual establishment as an indispensable medium in the musical life of the twentieth century. During the long period of eclipse Mozart's serenade *Eine kleine Nachtmusik* stands out as a famous exception; Mendelssohn's series of string symphonies is another, less famous but no less valuable artistically and historically. Chamber music for more than six solo stringed instruments is even rarer in the classical-romantic period. Works of the serenade type abound, but they are either for wind alone or, like Schubert's Octet of 1824, for a mixed group of wind and strings. Mendelssohn's Octet, written for four violins, two violas and two cellos, virtually brings into existence a new medium, and does so with such complete and triumphant skill that it has remained the only successful example of its genre, despite the attempts of Gade and Raff to emulate it. In its own age it towered above its most obvious rivals, Spohr's four double string quartets, which, lacking the spontaneity of the Mendelssohn work, are also self-limiting through their rigid division of the instruments into two conventionally organised quartets balanced against each other, whereas Mendelssohn can allow himself any permutations of the eight players.

While the Octet belongs legitimately to the realm of chamber music for solo instruments, Mendelssohn was conscious of its affinity to the string symphony in which he was an experienced practitioner, and had no purist qualms about implying this in the score: 'This Octet must be played by all the instruments in symphonic orchestral style. *Pianos* and *fortes* must be strictly observed and more strongly emphasised than is usual in pieces of this character.' He had, later on, to reconcile himself to the popu-

[1] See also p. 64.

larity of the scherzo as an independent piece, and added wind parts to it so that it could be used as an alternative to the minuet and trio of his C minor Symphony. In this form the scherzo became a favourite orchestral show-piece in England, particularly at the Crystal Palace concerts, where, Grove observed, 'like the scherzo of the Reformation Symphony, it rarely escapes an encore'.

The orchestral aspect is to the fore in the opening bars of the Octet, where tremolando and syncopated chords make a vibrant background to the soaring arpeggio theme of the first violin, which one can hardly doubt was written for Eduard Rietz, to whom the work is dedicated. This homogeneous texture, foreshadowing the E minor String Quartet, Op. 44, no. 2, and the Violin Concerto, also in that key, soon breaks up into more independent contrapuntal lines, and a new figure emerges in the shape of four staccato semiquavers. From this point the eight instruments are manipulated with a wealth of resource: now pairing one with another, as in the smooth second subject, which has been compared with the writing of Brahms in its use of sixths and double sixths and in the variety of its phrase-lengths; now contrasting registers – it is worth noticing how, with two violas and two cellos available, the composer does not overlook the special colour to be obtained from the lower range of the violin compass – and meanwhile demanding a full range of nuances in performance, and constantly varying the density of the scoring, from twelve-part chords to a single violin poised far above magically changing harmonies of violas and cellos, from the contrapuntal interweaving of motives to that supreme test of ensemble, rapid passages for all the instruments in unisons and octaves. Although so rich in material and so spacious in development, the form of this movement is admirably concise and logical, showing that the composer had left behind him some of the prolixities of the string symphonies.

The *andante* opens up even greater depths of imagination. In the opening bars, where the violas sound a bare fifth, the four lower instruments are contrasted with a quartet of violins, the two groups being opposed in keys a semitone apart. Again, harmony and modulation are rich and adventurous, with a perfectly proportioned use of chromaticism that is never allowed to overthrow the classic balance of key-relationships or, as happens too often in Spohr's chamber music, to weaken and sentimentalise. One more source of colour and vitality should be mentioned: the skilful use of doublings, a sure sign of the born string writer. The following shows one of the points at which effects of great beauty are obtained by this means:

Ex. 5

The scherzo represents Mendelssohn at his most imaginative, even in this type of movement he made so much his own. Beside it, the more frequently played scherzo from the *Midsummer Night's Dream* music, written eighteen years later, seems almost tame. The two pieces have this much in common, however: both are inspired by Shakespearian imagery. In the case of the Octet it is Shakespeare as re-created by Goethe, for the immediate source of Mendelssohn's fantasy is the Walpurgis Night episode in the first part of *Faust,* or more precisely the passage entitled 'Walpurgis

Night's Dream, or the Golden Wedding of Oberon and Titania'. According to Fanny Mendelssohn, her brother had in mind Goethe's lines from the end of this scene:

> Wolkenzug und Nebelflor
> Erhellen sich von oben.
> Luft im Laub und Wind im Rohr,
> Und alles ist zerstoben.
>
> *(Floating cloud and trailing mist*
> *Brightening o'er us hover.*
> *Air stirs the brake, the rushes shake,*
> *And all our pomp is over.)*

In Goethe's text the lines are marked 'Orchestra (*pianissimo*)', and Mendelssohn in his turn directs the scherzo to be played *sempre pp e staccato*. We have already noted the possibility that he also took hints from the E flat Quartet of Cherubini, whom with teenage candour he had described as being like an extinct volcano covered in stones and lava, but still capable of throwing out occasional flashes and sparks. If indeed some of the features of this and later scherzos were derived from so unexpected a source – the gossamer semiquavers, the economically placed pizzicatos, the high-pitched fanfares like miniature trumpets, the witty melodic inversions – Mendelssohn extended and improved on them with the vision of genius, sustaining and intensifying their imaginative potency throughout the long and complex movement. The breathless pace makes it difficult to concentrate on technical details: Fanny Mendelssohn, remembering perhaps Mephistopheles' question to Faust: 'Verlangst du nicht nach einem Besenstiele?', thought a broomstick would be the only way to keep up with it. One can only refer briefly to a few of the happiest devices: the way the movement is unified by using the same motive in the principal theme (introduced by the first violin) and simultaneously in diminution as accompaniment (second violin and first viola); the dazzling sevenfold imitations, overlapping at only two quavers' distance; the legato and staccato tremolandos for all the instruments together, giving a shimmering impressionistic effect; and the diamond-pointed unisons and octaves of the coda, with the first violin taking off in flight at the last moment. The finale is unique in its design, a daring amalgam of rondo and fugato. The closest analogy to it is the finale of Mozart's *Jupiter* Symphony, with its dazzling interplay of motives, some of which are scraps of traditional theme and counter-theme garnered from the contrapuntal workshops of the past. So classical is the structure of Mendelssohn's movement that it poses problems of interpretation; should the aim be an austere nobility of effect, or is there an underlying sense of comedy, even of mischief? The question arises at once with the fugal subject and answer, each made up of thirty *presto* quavers and a crotchet:

Ex. 6

Not even the best cellists can make this sound dignified, and unless one subscribes to the view that Mendelssohn has for once miscalculated an instrumental effect the only conclusion must be that the whole of this passage is humorous in intention. A possibility is that Mendelssohn's thoughts were still running either on the witches' sabbath of Goethe's Walpurgis Night scenes, or on Shakespeare's fantasy of the overlapping supernatural and mortal worlds. If the scherzo mirrors the court of Oberon and Titania, why should not the following movement be in some sense an expression of the other side of the comedy, with the grotesque antics of the tradesmen of Athens? In a year's time Mendelssohn was, at the age of seventeen, to 'begin to dream the *Midsummer Night's Dream* overture', where there is no doubt of the comic significance of the second-subject theme which might almost be regarded as a rhythmic variant of Ex. 6.

Whether we are right or not about this intention, there can be no mistake about the light hand with which a seemingly academic design is treated. The opening fugal exposition, for example, avoids an inexorable completeness by telescoping the entries of the violins and plunging onwards into one of the several counter-themes that combine with the busy quavers. Soon afterwards, contrapuntal activity is temporarily suspended in favour of a sturdy Beethovenish theme in fortissimo octaves; but this also is presently shorn of its dignity by having its reiterated notes distributed mockingly among the four violins – a joke that Beethoven himself would have been the first to appreciate. The first counter-theme also, which is basically identical with the notes set to 'And He shall reign for ever and ever' in *Messiah,* is put through its paces in ways that are far from reverential. As an example of telling string effects, one might single out the bars preceding the counter-exposition of the fugue subject, when the first violin starts on what is to become a lonely flight (of more than a hundred and thirty unbroken quavers), initially with the support of the other members of the ensemble, some pizzicato, others bowed, and the *second* cello off-side, as it were, clinging to a high F. The counter-exposition itself is no mechanical process. The instruments are paired off differently, and there is a new counter-theme constructed entirely from the notes of a common chord. From this point contrapuntal intricacy intensifies, with the working of all the rich and varied material already introduced and the addition of some new ideas. At the same time, modulation takes place on a spectacular scale, touching on keys far removed from the primary centres; yet all is done with such assurance that we are brought back to the tonic key at a moment when the master-stroke of the design can make its full effect. This is the return, sudden but quite unselfconscious, of the elfin scherzo theme, which immediately combines with the quavers of the finale subject and, more assertively, with the homophonic Beethovenish theme, and then disappears from the scene as quickly as it reappeared. Its very transience enhances the brilliance of this cyclic gesture, which is made to seem an inevitable part of the process of organic development. The movement swirls past it towards its final section, as if to echo Goethe's line, 'Und alles ist zerstoben': all vanishes into the golden dust of fairy pageantry.

The Earlier String Quartets and String Quintet

The earliest of the three string quartets Mendelssohn wrote in the key of E flat is dated by the autograph 25 March 1823, thus coming between the first and second piano quartets. Altogether this was a year of activity in the field of string composition. Several of the string symphonies were written at that time, most of them for the quintet combination with two violas, though the twelfth of the series, in G, uses the more normal two violins, viola, and 'bassi', and with its *adagio* introduction and fugal first movement looks forward to the String Quartet in A minor Op. 13. The 1823 Quartet, though published as long ago as 1879 by Erler of Leipzig, was never assigned a posthumous opus number and has remained almost unknown and unplayed. The autograph was bought in 1878 from a member of that firm and is now in the British Museum. A modern edition in miniature score is published by Ries and Erler of Berlin. Apart from demonstrating the composer's technical precocity and growing command of quartet style, the work has its own charm and by no means deserves to be left out of account. It remains, however, a student exercise, emphasising by its existence the tremendous leap forward in originality and command of the medium that took place from the beginning of the violin lessons with Rietz in 1824 and the visit to Paris in 1825. At this stage the treatment of the instruments is tentative; they are in fact almost restricted to the stave, and even the first violin part does not venture beyond the third position. In the prevalently conservative style, however, there are a few outbreaks, like the startling modulation out of the home key of E flat to the extremely remote A major, which occurs at the outset of the coda of the first movement, and the equally hazardous transition back to the tonic before an undistinguished, though competently written, ending. There is an even more uncertain groping for keys before the *da capo* of the minuet, as if the composer felt, not without justification, that he had stayed over-long in the tonic E flat, especially as the trio also had been in that key. The intervening *adagio non troppo* recalls Mozart in his melancholy 6/8 minor vein, and has some sound if not particularly original quartet writing. The finale is an unidiomatic exercise in fugue, doubtless one of the products of Zelter's rigorous course of contrapuntal study. The movement is in the form of a triple fugue, with two of the subjects exposed in the opening section. After a cadence on the dominant the third subject is introduced and gradually worked with the other two, most of the textbook devices of stretto, augmentation, and pedals being conscientiously employed. The writing of fugues for string quartet was one of the regular exercises Zelter prescribed; a number of Mendelssohn's schoolroom efforts of the kind survive among the unpublished manuscripts. A more elaborate and mature example, a double fugue – again in E flat – worked out with some feeling for string technique, found its way into the miscellany published as Op. 81. The manuscript of this movement is dated Berlin, 1 November 1827 – a few days after the completion of the

A minor Quartet, Op. 13, where contrapuntal erudition has become thoroughly integrated with the composer's expressive resources.

Mendelssohn's visit to Paris in company with his father in 1825 (actually his second visit – there had been an earlier one when Felix was only seven) proved a turning-point in his career, stimulating both his critical and his creative faculties. Nowhere else in Europe could a young musician have met with such a range of talent and variety of outlook as was represented by Cherubini, Rossini, Meyerbeer, Auber, Liszt, Berlioz, Hummel, Onslow the prolific and popular dilettante composer of quartets and quintets, Baillot the violinist and teacher of violinists, and Reicha, flautist, composer and theorist, who had been a colleague of Beethoven's in the Elector's orchestra at Bonn and was to number both Berlioz and César Franck among his pupils. Felix thrived on the praise that came his way for his B minor Piano Quartet and other early compositions, but still more on the technical brilliance of many of the artists he met, and the string players especially: Viotti and Rodolphe Kreutzer, Habeneck and Baillot. But far from overwhelming him with their authority, these renowned personalitites seemed to bring out the independence of his own character, so that he went out of his way to assert the claims of German music, especially J. S. Bach and Beethoven; like Spohr five years earlier, he reacted against the shallowness of much of the operatic, church, and salon music the French admired. He even found faults in the extemporisation of Liszt, the orchestration of Auber, and the operas of Rossini. When he returned from Paris it was with intellect and imagination stirred, but at the same time with a renewed faith in the solid virtues of the German classical tradition, with its bias towards instrumental music, that his early training, alike in music as in history and philosophy, had given him.

He was eighteen when he wrote the A minor Quartet. If the manuscript score in the British Museum is in Mendelssohn's autograph, as there is no reason to doubt, the very appearance of the notes on paper suggests that they were written down with a young man's energy and at the dictation of a brain teeming with ideas. The calligraphy, though clear and elegant as always with Mendelssohn, whether in scores or letters, is here unusually bold, even dashing. Occasionally bars are erased, giving greater concision, while the very expression marks, in their profusion and exactness, register composition at a high temperature. Strangely enough, it was the third quartet assured of immortality to be written round the same keynote in the space of a few years. Schubert, at the age of thirty, seems to have heard the first performance of his most lovable and perhaps his finest Quartet, also in A minor, Op. 29, in the year of Mendelssohn's Paris visit. And Beethoven, near the close of his life, had composed his great A minor Quartet, Op. 132, only two years before Mendelssohn's Op. 13. Although it was not published until the end of 1827, there can be little doubt that Mendelssohn knew it; the thematic similarities in the first movements can hardly be accidental.

At Whitsuntide, 1827, Mendelssohn had set some lines by J. G. Droyson (known as 'Voss') as a short single-strophe song, 'Frage', Op. 9, no. 1, 'Is it true that you are always waiting for me in the arboured walk?':

Ex. 7   FRAGE [*Question*]

The three-note questioning motive, with its characteristic rhythmic shape, became the motto theme of the String Quartet finished on 26 October in the same year. The motto lies at the heart of the *adagio* introduction and returns, in more extended and explicit form, at the close of the whole Quartet, thus framing it with matching but not identical prologue and epilogue. But the cyclic principle goes further than this. It is hardly an exaggeration to say that the whole of the Quartet grows out of the introductory *adagio,* and that the motto theme and its derivatives are seldom long absent from any part of the work. There is nothing obvious or forced about this process; in fact, it is concealed at the outset of the *allegro vivace* by a change of mode (major to minor) and a change of metre (triple to quadruple). The preliminary scurry of semiquavers at this point is also deceptive; not only is it derived from the radical motive, but it eventually turns out to have important thematic functions of its own. Of still greater importance is the principal subject of the movement, introduced by the viola and imitated in turn by the other three instruments. Its relation to the 'Ist es wahr?' theme is made obvious in the rhythm, while the significance of the viola counter-theme is even greater:

Ex. 8

The form of the *allegro vivace* is broadly that of a classical first movement, the establishment of E minor as the secondary key being marked by an impassioned melody for the cello – a theme again derived from the basic idea. The texture of the movement is almost entirely contrapuntal, with writing at a level of dissonance it is hard to parallel from any other music of the period, excepting only the Beethoven late quartets. Those who might think it absurd to mention in the same breath a work by Mendelssohn and Wagner's *Tristan* (written thirty years later) should consider such a passage as the following, taken almost at random from the movement under discussion (and this is mild in comparison with what happens in the *adagio non lento*):

Ex. 9

Mendelssohn knew he was being revolutionary at this time, and never more so than in this Quartet, as we know from his remarks about its success with the Parisian avant-garde. But it did not please the staid English critic Chorley, who looked back upon it from that rather less than glorious era of English musical life, the 1850s:

Some hard and dry and (as he called them) 'rebellious' compositions were put forth in his young days . . . These were the works of a boy anxious to prove himself a man among the double refined intelligences of those by whom he was surrounded; and parading his science, his knowledge of the ancients, his mastery over all the learning of his Art. Year by year, less aridity, more grace, flexibility, and versatility, marked the thinking and writing of Mendelssohn. There is the distance of a long life betwixt his early String Quartet in A minor with the *Lied* prefixed, and his last Quintet in B flat . . .

The reference to 'knowledge of the ancients' evidently means Mendelssohn's enthusiasm for the music of J. S. Bach, which had resulted shortly before Chorley was writing in the foundation of the *Bach-Gesellschaft*. Eduard Devrient, in his recollections of Mendelssohn, described how he used to sing with Felix and Fanny in the Berlin Singakademie 'what Zelter called the "bristly pieces" of Sebastian Bach', and how, in the winter of 1827 – immediately following the completion of the Quartet in A minor, therefore – Felix began to rehearse the *St Matthew Passion* with a small select choir. As for Chorley's preference for the B flat Quintet, few would now be found to agree with him.

To revert to the first movement of the Quartet, the beginning of the development is signalled by a renewed surging of the semiquaver figures – anticipating on a small scale the *Fingal's Cave* Overture to be written a few years later – and continues with another passage of intensive contrapuntal working, with the upper instruments in canon. The recapitulation is made an exciting process in which the events of the exposition are reviewed rather than re-enacted; the quartet writing here is outstandingly fine in its clarity and sonority. The coda brings some slackening of the sense of tension and strenuous effort, displaying the principal theme in a warm harmonic setting.

The second movement (*adagio non lento* – the tempo directions in this work show great scrupulosity) is even more heavily charged, both emotionally and intellectually, and presents an intricate pattern of organisation. In a strange and subtle way it is a micro-cosm of the whole Quartet, being framed between two free yet identifiable paraphrases of the *Lied*. The first of these, in F major, is followed by a *fugato* in D minor, full of dark chromatic progressions of the kind associated with the more poignant fugues in Bach's *Forty-eight*. The subject of the *fugato* is given to the viola, and is recognisable as a variant of Ex. 8. The counterpoint of this section reaches new heights of expressive dissonance. The atmosphere lightens momentarily in a brief scherzando, where the first violin, eloquent above a gently throbbing accompaniment, seems to remember the second subject of the previous movement. The more fluid rhythm thus set up continues through a stressful development of the fugal theme, which now reappears in an inverted form, until at the climax the original direction prevails. From this point the tension eases off again, to reach, through a short violin cadenza, the final *Lied*-paraphrase. The whole extraordinary movement ends with a coda, where the *fugato* theme is dismissed with a mingling of wit and tenderness, contrapuntal science and sensuous beauty.

The intermezzo, in whose opening melodic contours the basic motive again asserts itself, can best be described as an attractive tune of the *Volkslied* kind, charmingly simple and delicately scored – a perfect foil to the sophisticated movements that have gone before. There is a central section which moves at a quicker pace; the British Museum manuscript shows that the composer changed his mind at least twice about the speed, marking it first *più presto,* then *un poco più mosso,* and finally erasing both in favour of *allegro di molto*. It is in effect a miniature scherzo, calling for featherweight refinements of legato and staccato bowing. Towards the end, viola and cello seem to insist on drawing attention to the fundamental identity of this ethereal movement with the underlying motive of the rest of the work.

The finale (*presto*) starts with a dramatic gesture in D minor, the first violin declaiming an impassioned recitative above tremolando chords. Once more thematic resemblances begin to crowd in; the violin's opening phrase is a version of Ex. 8, and the connecting imitative passages are built on a motive of slurred quavers which soon becomes a prominent feature and is also clearly related to some of the first-movement material. Dramatic suspense is intensified by the instability of the key-scheme; beginning in D minor, it drops to C, then rises again to D major and minor. Not until the twenty-ninth bar is the tonic key of A minor established. With it comes a principal subject that once again seems to indicate an indebtedness to Beethoven's Op. 132. Apropos a performance of his own Op. 13 in a Paris salon, Mendelssohn tells a story of being addressed by one of the guests, the Abbé Bardin: 'At the last movement my neighbour pulled my coat, and said, "Il a cela dans une de ses sinfonies." "Qui?" said I, rather embarrassed. "Beethoven, l'auteur de ce quatuor," said he, with a consequential air. This was bitter sweet!' The similarities between the Beethoven and Mendelssohn finales extend to the harmonies and rhythms of the accompanying parts. Mendelssohn's theme begins suavely, but this mood does not continue; harsh suspensions, restless quaver movement with distant allusions to the all-pervading basic motive, and emphatic accentuation culminate in a powerfully rhetorical half-cadence on the dominant of E minor and the reintroduction of the recitative motive – which we now realise to be an inverted form of the fugato subject – and another burst of dramatic energy, leading in its turn to an uncompromisingly formal cadence in E minor. This marks the end of the exposition. With the last chord of the cadence, the fugato subject re-enters on the viola, and is treated in serene three-part counterpoint by the upper instruments, while the cello, biding its time, begins to raise to the surface its own variant of the same motive. Gradually the whole fabric is lifted up and by the same process of motival integration united with the prevailing tempo of the movement. The turning-point of the drama is a violent octave passage in quavers (marked *non ligato*) leading to another outburst of recitative, a brief recapitulation of the principal theme, a lamenting farewell to the *fugato* subject by the first violin above a tremolando accompaniment, and last fleeting references to the rondo theme and the slow movement: the score marks this *a piacere quasi una fantasia* (though the autograph has clearly . . . *quasi non fantasia*). The first violin, alone, sets the stage for the final episode, the return of the major key and the postlude founded on 'Ist es wahr?' Now the connection with the *Lied* becomes explicit, with a note-for-note quotation to round off the whole work: 'she who feels with me and stays ever true to me'. No other string quartet had ever been organised in this way, even by Beethoven, and as with the Octet, the model is both unique and unrepeatable.

Although the Quartet in E flat, Op. 12, bears an earlier opus number, it was written two years after the Quartet in A minor.

The autograph bears the finishing date 'London, Sept. 14: 1829'; in a letter addressed to his sisters four days earlier, Mendelssohn wrote that he was in the middle of the last movement, and had also finished an organ piece for Fanny's wedding. The Quartet thus belongs to the happy and fertile period of Mendelssohn's tour of Scotland and Wales, a journey that was also to provide inspiration for two major orchestral works, the *Fingal's Cave* overture and the Scottish Symphony.

Though far from conventional in structure, the E flat Quartet makes fewer demands on performers and listeners than its strenuous predecessor. Indebtedness to Beethoven is again in evidence, especially in the opening bars:

Ex. 10

which immediately invite comparison with the 'Harp' Quartet, Op. 74, likewise an *adagio* in E flat. The close resemblances between rhythmic shapes and melodic intervals should not, however, be allowed to distract attention from the widely different ways in which the two works subsequently develop.

Mendelssohn is still interested in cyclic methods of construction. He does not repeat his former procedure of bringing back his introductory *adagio* at the end of the work, but he does create a kind of cyclic pattern by later references to this introduction, as well as by a return, towards the close of the Quartet, of the tuneful theme that opens the *allegro non tardante*. This same suave melody gives rise to a subsidiary theme, heard sometimes with and sometimes without an upbeat, but invariably associated with the key of F minor (the supertonic); it first occurs in the development of the first movement, reappears in the coda, and is heard once more (still in F minor) in the coda of the finale. It is worth noticing that the development begins with a false *da capo*, the first subject being restated at this point as though there were to be a repeat of the entire exposition in the earlier classical tradition; there is a well-known precedent for Mendelssohn's procedure in the first movement of Beethoven's F major Quartet, Op. 59, no. 1. One moment not to be missed is that preceding the return of the principal theme at the recapitulation, where the widely spaced translucent texture seems like the perfect musical counterpart of Mendelssohn's exquisite pencil and water-colour sketches:

Ex. 11

If I may repeat what I have written elsewhere, 'the entire movement diffuses a sense of tranquillity and almost physical well-being'.

The canzonetta corresponds to the intermezzo of Op. 13. Again we have a folksong-like melody with a more animated, scherzo type of middle section in the major mode. Its simplicity and its attractive scoring, with the telling use of pizzicato and sustained notes, have long made it the most popular of all Mendelssohn's quartet movements. In some ways it closely resembles the familiar G major-minor dance from Schubert's *Rosamunde* music. The *andante espressivo,* though beginning very much like the slow movement of Op. 13, is much less elaborate, being in simple *Lied* form and quite brief. It is stamped, however, with the identity of the Quartet; the first and most often repeated phrase of the melody, with its three ascending quavers, is related to the introductory *adagio non troppo.*

This *andante* is in the key of B flat major. The finale (*molto allegro e vivace*) follows hard upon it, not in the expected tonic of the work, E flat, but in the relative C minor, and this proves to be the central key throughout almost the whole movement, while even the secondary keys (chiefly dominant and subdominant) are minor. It is only at the coda that there is an abrupt swing back to E flat major, and this is brought about in an unconventional way. First the metre changes from the previous 12/8 to a simple quadruple, and the quartet reiterates, in the manner of a fanfare or march, the rhythm of the opening *adagio*. This outburst soon subsides into a short recitative for the first violin, which first inverts the theme of the opening *adagio,* then hints at the recurrent F minor theme from the first movement. This is taken up unanimously, and leads to the long-deferred return of the principal theme of the *allegro non tardante.* The coda of this finale is one of Mendelssohn's purest and most radiant passages of quartet writing, leaving the listener with a wonderful sense of contentment.

The Quintet for Strings in A came into being at the same period as these two string quartets, having been originally composed in 1826; but the version published as Op. 18, with the impassioned intermezzo in memory of Eduard Rietz, dates from 1832. Rietz died in the January of that year. He had been Mendelssohn's teacher for the violin and one of his closest friends, the inspiration of much of his work, the dedicatee of the Octet, and one of his right-hand men in the Bach revival. The intermezzo, inscribed 'Nachruf' (In memoriam), was intended both as a farewell to Rietz and also as a tribute to the violinist who came second only to him in Mendelssohn's esteem, Pierre Marie Baillot. Completed a month after Rietz's death, it replaced the scherzo as second movement, and the scherzo supplanted a minuet and trio which were discarded altogether.

Mendelssohn follows Mozart in adopting the quintet combination with two violas, and the spirit of Mozart seems to linger in the opening pages of this work (there is even a recollection of the second trio of Mozart's Clarinet Quintet in the same key). The overlapping entries in the second paragraph contribute to this impression: in fact, the melodic outline that results is none other than the classic four-note theme of the *Jupiter* finale, about whose merits Mendelssohn once engaged in a friendly dispute; he was to use the formula again in the Reformation Symphony. The exposition is repeated. In the development there is much delightful counterpoint which, however complex it becomes, never leads to congestion or heaviness. Even in passages – and they are fairly extensive – where the first violin appears to be dominating the ensemble, it will generally be found that the other parts have some unobtrusive interest of their own.

The concertante style of the violin writing in the intermezzo has obvious justification in view of the two artists it commemorates. It exploits the full range of the instrument, in a way more characteristic of a concerto than a solo ensemble, yet it remains within chamber-music style, with richly independent part-writing, particularly in the cello line. The impressiveness of such sonorous polyphony is enhanced by the freedom of modulation which the large scale of the movement permits to be carried out at leisure. This movement is certainly the emotional peak of the Quintet, as it was intended to be.

The scherzo is likewise broad in design, and a splendid example of fugal texture handled with wit and delicacy. Mendelssohn's scherzos are always unmistakably his own, but in this particular case he seems to draw added vitality from two great predecessors: Beethoven, who in the scherzo of his early C minor Quartet, Op. 18, no. 4, and again in the second movement of the first Razumovsky Quartet, Op. 59, no. 1, makes similar play with repeated-note figures; and Bach, whose fugal preludes to the English Suites generate motor rhythms and develop them imitatively over wide time-spans. The sustained virtuosity of Mendelssohn's five-part counterpoint, both in the stricter fugato passages and in the freer episodes, might well qualify him for the title of Bach's aptest pupil. But it would be a mistake to overlook the un-Bachian happenings, and particularly the points where the brakes are applied; one of these moments occurs before the final stretto, with a series of sustained harmonies laid out impressionistically to take advantage of viola tone-colour:

Ex. 12

The rearrangement of movements in the revised form of the Quintet created certain problems of balance. Now that the brilliant scherzo stands as the penultimate movement, it must inevitably detract from the full effectiveness of the finale (*allegro vivace*), which also is of scherzo-like character and contains a good deal of imitative writing. None the less it has its own individuality, helped by lively syncopations and a fine broad tune that again arouses memories of Beethoven's first Razumovsky: there is a faint resemblance between Mendelssohn's theme and the Russian folksong in the finale of the Beethoven work. In general style, however, Mendelssohn comes even closer to an earlier Beethoven movement, the finale of the Quartet in F, Op. 18, no. 1. The family likeness can be seen in the triplet semiquavers, the staccato quavers, and the wide rising intervals, to mention only a few common features.

The String Quartets, Op. 44

The years from 1831 onwards, following his travels in Britain, Italy and Switzerland, were for Mendelssohn a period of increasing fame and public responsibilities. A life of enviable creative and social freedom was now to be replaced by an incessant round of performing, conducting, administering cultural and educational schemes, and writing to order for festivals, with all the travelling between the major centres – Berlin, Paris, Leipzig, Düsseldorf, and London – these activities entailed. He was the first great creative musician in history to feel the effects of such pressures, which are now only too well known to the modern artist. The drain on his nervous resources was severe, and in the long run much of the spontaneity and adventurousness of his earlier compositions, including the chamber music, shows a decline. This was no sudden process, however, and there is happily little evidence of it in the group of three string quartets written in the years 1837-8 and published as Op. 44. They are often regarded, indeed, as the crown of his achievement in this medium.

The first to be written was the E minor, Op. 44, no. 2. The autograph is dated 18 June 1837, and thus belongs to the contented and musically productive period following its composer's marriage to Cécile Jeanrenaud. The first performance was given by Ferdinand

David's quartet at the Leipzig Gewandhaus on 17 November in the same year. The key of E minor had a special attraction for Mendelssohn; he was to use it again in a year or so for his second and best-known Violin Concerto, whose opening is foreshadowed in the soaring melody of the first violin at the beginning of the Quartet. Another feature to be noticed is the falling seventh which, inverted, recurs in the finale. Although firmly unified, the first movement contains a remarkable variety of material and texture, passages of mainly vertical interest being relieved by counterpoint, unison passages by imitative dialogue, and so on, these different elements being welded together with cunning craftsmanship and exhilarating effect. The rising arpeggio in crotchets that opens the movement gives rise to figures in quaver-diminution, and these become an important integrating factor. Another thematic element is the flight of pianissimo semiquavers which appears first in unisons and octaves, and soon shows itself to be a source of contrapuntal figuration throughout the movement. The recapitulation of the main theme, often one of the best moments in a Mendelssohn work, is achieved in this case by making the arpeggio figures, in both their crotchet and diminished forms, ever more insistent until they escort the theme back into the tonic key and then remain about it as a more active replacement for the syncopated accompaniment of the original statement.

Several other aspects of this movement deserve attention. The G major melody serving as second subject is, like the corresponding theme in the Op. 12 Quartet, a derivative of the principal E minor theme. The two ideas may, as it were, be regarded as the masculine and feminine aspects of the same motive. In the development section the main first-subject themes already mentioned – the rising arpeggio and the semiquaver runs – are worked together with great strength and economy. So vital and original is the form of this movement, however, that it would be unrealistic to think of development as being confined to the central section. Further aspects of the material are explored, for example, after the recapitulation of the second-subject theme (in E major), with a disposition of parts – viola holding the tonic as a foundation, violins in the middle but with their normal positions reversed, and cello highest of all – that yields yet another example of the composer's insight into the quartet medium and the infinitude of sound combinations it can give rise to. Another phase of development comes in the coda, which is full of beautiful and ingenious ideas. Towards the end the second-subject tune is allowed quietly to show (in the submediant C major) its affinity to the main theme, after which the crotchet and quaver forms of that theme bring the movement to its end in a swelling fanfare.

In the scherzo Mendelssohn produces yet another example of his inexhaustible invention in devising movements of this type, each strongly individualised. Rather unusually, this one is in triple time, though no vestige of minuet style remains. Again, homophonic passages are intermingled with linear imitative treatment, the motive of four repeated semiquavers acting as a unifying common factor. Energy is generated here not merely by speed and continuity of movement, but also by the thrust of contrapuntal stresses. An unexpected detail is the appearance, just before the main theme returns, of a new and graceful melody for the viola, straying in and retreating almost at once, as if half apologetically. No other instrument is allowed to touch this theme, but the viola has it again, in more confidently extended form and in the major, near the end of the movement. The final cadence, with its upward arpeggios, hints at the opening of the Quartet.

The *andante* is a song without words, protected against sentimentality by the direction that it must on no account be dragged (*schleppend*). The scoring of the opening recalls that of Schubert's A minor Quartet. The violin melody draws attention, in its third bar, to the arpeggio link with the main theme of the first movement. On its return this melody is reassigned to the cello on its A string, the viola now providing the bass. A subsidiary theme introduces rhythmic variety, while incorporating the arpeggio motive, and contributes another example of the kind of harmonic roughness that Mendelssohn is not afraid of when it is the outcome of a logical progression of parts:

Ex. 13

The unprepared major ninths at the final cadence are also unusual in the context of the period, and are finely placed.

There could hardly be clearer evidence of the superiority of Mendelssohn's chamber music over much of his other work, both vocal and instrumental, than the finale of this Quartet presents. In one of his piano pieces, for example, this *presto agitato* opening would not be out of place, but we might forecast its subsequent course as little more than a facile exploitation of a promising idea. Writing in the quartet medium, on the other hand, Mendelssohn brings into play his full powers of construction and expression. In general, we may say that his piano writing represents his public image, while the chamber music reveals the inner thoughts and feelings of the man. The first bar establishes a thematic relationship with the arpeggio motive of the first movement, while the second subject is dominated by a tune whose rising contours emphasise the underlying identity of the two movements. The leaping seventh of this melody, already referred to, recalls the use of the same interval, though in the opposite direction, in the first movement. Yet another free variant of this tune appears in the course of the development, and incidentally takes part in an adroit modulation from G to F major. One is reminded, as not infrequently in Mendelssohn's chamber music, of the elliptical transitions of Fauré:

Ex. 14

This quotation illustrates the colour-effects produced in this movement by doubling a line at the octave; here the doubling is between the two violins, but elsewhere doublings of one or other violin with viola also occur. The reduction in number of real parts at such moments can create a spare linear texture seldom met with in quartet writing at this period. As a whole, the E minor Quartet demonstrates that the composer had reached a stage of equilibrium in his treatment of the classical forms. Each movement of the Quartet is cast in some variety of sonata form, and he has begun to restrain his earlier inclinations towards cylic procedures, and his attempts to amalgamate sonata and fugue. Even unification by motive, though far from being discarded, is now used more subtly and unobtrusively.

Yet there is still a strongly progressive, if not revolutionary, spirit in the next of the Op. 44 Quartets in order of composition, no. 3 in E flat. This was completed on 6 February 1838. The cyclic principle is at work here too; not only the first movement, but the third and fourth also are unified by means of the figure of four semiquavers forming the upbeat to the first bar of the work, while the scherzo has its own methods of integration involving fugal procedures. The first movement unfolds from the material in the opening bars of a long-breathed paragraph, whose two related motives *a* and *b* will be found to pervade almost every bar of the movement:

Ex. 15

The four-note motive serves both as the kernel of the development and also as a connecting idea to link the successive stages of the movement; for example, it accompanies the introduction of the second-subject theme, which is itself derived from Ex. 15*b*. The climactic use of the four-note group at the start of the recapitulation again shows the composer's flair for making this an exciting point in his sonata-form movements. Harmonically, also, there is much to admire. The modulations occurring during the introduction of the second subject are particularly elegant: instead of going straight to the dominant key, B flat major, there are transitions to the relative and tonic minors of that key (G minor and B flat minor), and thence by way of D flat major and F minor to the 'dominant of the dominant', F major. This ease in modulating freely, without the excessive aid of recondite chromatic or enharmonic means, is one that Mendelssohn acquired early in his career. At the same time, this movement shows a bold use of contrary streams of parallel intervals without regard to the dissonances produced. There are plenty of precedents for such heterophony in Bach and Beethoven, but its occurrence in the 1830s must be exceptional. The coda is not the least interesting part of this movement, throwing new light on the material and creating some rare effects of sonority; the score is here delicately coloured by pizzicato chords and fourth-string writing for violins and viola.

The scherzo in C minor is romantic woodland music, a genre that no German composer from Weber to Brahms was able to resist. The horse-hooves and hunting-calls of Brahms's E flat Trio, Op. 40, have been anticipated here, almost thirty years earlier. But Mendelssohn is no more satisfied than Brahms with a mere descriptive sound-picture. The hunting-rhythms of the first part of the scherzo break off suddenly, to be succeeded by a light-weight fugato introduced by the viola, which maintains the same sense of movement, though with more fragmentary articulation. After a modified recapitulation of the main 'hunting' section (for this is an extended movement of rondo type), a second fugato episode occurs, varied this time by the addition of a chromatic counter-theme, drawn like a coloured thread into the texture. On the final reappearance of the principal theme it seems momentarily to have adopted the fugato tendency, but the counterpoint quickly coalesces into a single unison line (literally unison, not octaves) and then spreads out again chromatically to reach a pizzicato and piano ending to one of the most imaginative and finely wrought of the composer's scherzos.

The *adagio* in A flat is a warm-hearted outpouring of romantic feeling, expressed in *Lied*-form. Thematically it is linked with both first and last movements, chiefly by means of the four-note anacrusis. Harmonically, Mendelssohn shows that he is behind none of his contemporaries in freedom of modulation and the use of expressive dissonance: such a passage as this may have a touch of Spohr in the chromatic cadence, but as a whole it is more suggestive of Schumann, whose chamber music was as yet unwritten:

Ex. 16

The undulating figure of accompaniment becomes of greater importance in the middle section of the movement, where it is luxuriantly intertwined with a two-crotchet motive extracted (by inversion) from the opening theme. At the end of the movement the first violin twice quotes the semiquaver arpeggio, thereby looking both backwards and forwards, since without hesitation the same figure is adopted as the starting-point of the finale (*molto allegro con fuoco*). Here the composer meets his usual problem – how to add the fourth movement that tradition exacts to three that have already exploited a great variety of tempi, textures, and thematic devices. Almost inevitably there is some feeling of anti-climax; yet there is a great deal more than animated bustle in this finale. The semiquaver motive may, it is true, be somewhat over-worked, but Mendelssohn also contrives to make other and more subtle allusions to the three preceding movements: the cantabile flow of the first, for example, is felt here also, as are the staccato repeated chords of the scherzo. At the same time, the movement develops features of its own, like the octave leaps which are sometimes comically overshot by the upper instruments until as in bars 41-3 of the recapitulation the cello gets them right.

On 30 July 1838 Mendelssohn wrote from Berlin to Ferdinand David, the violinist:

I have just finished my third Quartet, in D major, and like it much. I hope it may please you as well. I rather think it will, since it is more spirited and seems to me likely to be more grateful to the players than the others.

The same letter mentions that an E minor Violin Concerto is 'running through his head'. The Quartet is again referred to, along with other works completed or contemplated, in a letter to Hiller dated 17 August 1838. Mendelssohn says he very much likes the first movement, and especially a *forte* passage near the end. He has also finished a Cello Sonata and a Violin Sonata, and hopes to write 'a couple of trios'. The opening of the Violin Concerto, which Mendelssohn complained, 'gave him no peace', had already been adumbrated in the E minor Quartet; and its arpeggio character is shared also with the opening of the new Quartet in D. Mendelssohn finished the Quartet on 24 July 1838, and it was performed in public for the first time, at the Leipzig Gewandhaus, by the David quartet. The composer's particular fondness for it may have been the reason why it was the first of the set to appear in print. Not everyone will agree with Mendelssohn's judgment on this point; of all his quartets it is, perhaps, the most chastely classical, with few traces of the experimental tendencies of the earlier chamber works. It looks back to Haydn rather than Beethoven, and even has a minuet as its second movement. The other movements are in sonata form, though only the first has a full development section.

The composer's reference to the satisfaction he believes the players will find in it is understandable. The writing is throughout idiomatic and divides the interest fairly among the instruments. The Quartet 'plays' well; firmly based harmonic passages and linear writing in thirds are among the prominent features making for security in ensemble and brightness of effect, especially in this most resonant of string keys. The thematic material of the first movement is well contrasted, the principal subject being exuberant while the secondary theme, introduced obliquely in the relative minor of its central key (the dominant, A), moves more gravely by close intervals. The exposition has the traditional double bar and repeat. The development is elaborate, concerning itself not only with the vigorous initial theme but also with the smooth linking figures which lend themselves so well to contrapuntal treatment. The recapitulation and coda are more conventional than in the earlier quartets and bring no surprises.

The smoothness and euphony of the first movement characterise also the Haydnesque *minuetto*, with its part-writing in thirds and sixths and its elegant cadence extensions. The minor-mode trio falls into three sections, the outer ones picturesquely harmonised

46

over drone basses in the manner of the baroque musette, the central one of more linear interest. The key of B minor returns with the *andante espressivo con moto,* a lyrical movement of exceptional beauty, filled with wistful melody repeated with subtle harmonic variations and counter-melodies. Again Fauré comes to mind, and especially the haunting cadences of his orchestral *Pavane.* There is in both pieces a similar sense of nostalgia for a romanticised past, both are fastidiously wrought, and both are really salon music raised to the highest level of intelligence and refinement.

The finale is a whirling, headlong saltarello, akin to the one that rounds off the Italian Symphony, but adapted to chamber music style. It is brilliant entertainment music, with no pretensions to sophistication, and frankly availing itself of the repetitions and sequences acceptable on such conditions. But there is also a great deal of deft and witty musicianship at work behind the glittering façade. The principal subject, for example, is made up of three distinct motives which can follow on one another or, as soon happens, be combined contrapuntally. Canonic imitation is used plentifully, and Mendelssohn is as resourceful as ever in his modulations. The speed indicated – *presto con brio,* $\d=104$ – calls for the highest degree of technical finish and complete assurance on the part of the performers.

Later Works for Solo Strings with Piano

Except for the rediscovered Sonata in F for violin and piano (no opus number), these are all cello works. The Violin Sonata is contemporary with the Op. 44 Quartets, having been composed in 1838. Why it should have remained unpublished until 1953, when Yehudi Menuhin edited it for Peters, is one of the many mysteries that surround the motives of Mendelssohn's earlier publishers and literary executors. Technically the work shows a great advance on the early F minor Sonata, Op. 4, and it includes one superb movement, the *adagio.* Menuhin, who had previously brought to light the composer's first Concerto for Violin and Strings of 1822, refers in his edition of the Sonata to the 'ideal violin writing of Mendelssohn, as evidenced in the two Concerti and chamber music works'.

The first of the three movements (*allegro vivace*) starts, like a gavotte, on the second half of the bar. The bold, if not very distinguished, principal theme, is extended sequentially, and there is also much sequential treatment in the development. When the violin takes over the theme it is accompanied by arpeggios of a kind commonly used by the composer in his *Songs without Words* and piano variations. The second subject creates a special point of interest by modulating out of C into A flat, with a syncopated accompaniment.

The *adagio* is the best part of the work. It sets out with a splendid nine-bar theme, expressively coloured by diatonic seventh chords, beginning:

Ex. 17

This is developed, with great warmth of feeling, almost without interruption except where some new material occurs in a D minor – A minor episode; soon afterwards the principal theme returns, and is finally combined with the episodic material in a fine coda. The finale, *allegro vivace,* is a long and elaborate scherzo-like movement, calling for spiccato bowing. The instruments exchange ideas constantly, with easily flowing counterpoint. This is duo-writing of a mature quality, involving the partners on equal terms.

Mendelssohn made substantial contributions to the literature of the cello. He became interested in the instrument when his brother Paul took it up, and he had clearly studied Beethoven's five great sonatas, the first to solve the problems of balance between cello and piano. To begin with the least weighty of Mendelssohn's cello works, the posthumously published *Lied ohne Worte,* Op. 109, is a useful occasional piece, well written for the cello and exploiting its compass in upper and bass registers, though technically un-demanding. The piano part begins in rather a trite manner, but becomes more imaginative in the middle section, with a strongly moving bass and a neat return to the main key.

The *Variations concertantes,* Op. 17, are again in D major. They were written in January 1828 and dedicated to Paul Mendelssohn-Bartholdy. Mendelssohn seldom disappoints us when writing in variation form, and this work is extremely well constructed, justifying its ambitious title by making full use of the technical resources of both instruments. The theme is shared between them, with the cello supplying a bass to the piano when not itself engaged with the tune. With the first variation, the repeats of the binary theme are discarded and the cello plays it against a finger-staccato piano counterpoint. In Variation 2, the piano paraphrases the theme more freely, while the cello adds an interesting bass and makes occasional thematic allusions. Some new harmonic colouring is added in Variation 3, with the cello contributing elaborate figuration over a wide range of pitch. The chief interest of Variation 4 is in the piano part, but in Variation 5 energetic dialogue develops, staccato chords for the piano alternating with cello pizzicato. In Variation 6 the piano resumes the original rhythmic pattern of the theme while transforming both melody and harmony; meanwhile the cello adds a flowing counter-melody in semi-quavers. Variation 7 is freely extended in the minor mode, includes a brilliant passage in broken octaves for the piano alone, and ends quietly with a recitative for cello, which comes to rest on the dominant and prolongs it as a pedal bass for a restatement of the theme by the piano. An imposing coda involves both instruments in elaborate figuration.

Schumann gave the B flat Sonata for cello and piano, Op. 45, special praise for its purity as abstract music, while suggesting that it might be best enjoyed in the family circle after a reading of poetry by Goethe or Byron. Like the Variations, it was written for Paul Mendelssohn, though at a later date; it was completed on 13 October 1838, and is therefore contemporary with the F major Violin Sonata. The composer had learnt much from Beethoven, whose A major Cello Sonata, Op. 69, makes its influence felt in Mendelssohn's opening bars. There is a careful avoidance of over-harmonisation, a plentiful use of spare linear texture, with much two- and three-part writing to allow the cello to be audible in all its registers, and a fair distribution of the tasks of providing the fundamental bass. The themes themselves are admirable; Mendelssohn excelled in giving grateful melodies to the cello in all his instrumental music: the second subjects of the *Fingal's Cave* and *Ruy Blas* Overtures are familiar examples.

The middle movement is a melancholy autumnal *andante,* pervaded by a falling melodic figure, like a sigh of resignation; it resembles a slower and minor-mode version of the principal theme of Beethoven's Piano Sonata in E flat, Op. 31, no. 3. This motive unifies the outer and middle sections of the movement. After another broad cantabile melody for the cello, the return to the opening mood brings with it keyboard figuration of a kind rather unusual with Mendelssohn, while the cello makes effective use of pizzicato. The movement is extended by means of a coda with some interesting thematic development and further exploitation of antiphonal dialogue. The finale, *allegro assai,* suffers under the disadvantage of being too close to the first movement in speed and thematic character; to follow up Schumann's hint, the atmosphere tends towards a cosy domesticity. It is undeniably well laid out for the instruments, however, and most enjoyable for both players, while the listener can not only relax in the mellow sunlight of the composer's most Italianate manner but also gain some mental stimulation from the point where, in a G minor episode, the piano entirely transforms the suave main theme into a vigorous dance.

The second Sonata for cello and piano, in D, Op. 58, is a bigger and more grandiose work altogether, in four movements. It was composed during 1842-3 for Count Mateusz Wielhorski, a member of a highly musical Polish-Russian family. The Count was a pupil of Bernhard Romberg and possessed a Stradivarius cello which he eventually passed on to Karl Davidov. If one were to judge only by their first movements, this Sonata might seem, by comparison with its predecessor, altogether too facile and lacking in inventive power. The jaunty principal theme, built on the chord of D major in 6/8 time, contributes to this impression, though it suits the cello well and lends itself to development later. It is only with the two middle movements that Mendelssohn's imagination seems to come to life. The *allegretto scherzando* is filled with wit and humour. The pianist is called upon for a variety of staccato and legato touches and has a passage of thunderous octaves at the recapitulation: in the major-mode central section the cellist alternates pizzicato and arco in various registers. The main theme assumes a fresh aspect at each repetition, with well-timed points of imitation.

The *adagio* is one of Mendelssohn's most original movements. It takes the form of a chorale-like theme, which does not seem to be identifiable as coming from any of the traditional sources; nor does it suggest any relevance to the musical background of a Polish nobleman – Schumann tactfully gave him a mazurka-like tune to play on his cello in the corresponding movement of the piano quartet dedicated to him. Mendelssohn spreads the chorale over the keyboard in massive chords, bonded by the damper pedal and by the cello reinforcing the bass, so that an organ-like sound results. Between the phrases of the chorale the cello interpolates passages of quasi-recitative. Later the chorale and the cellist's commentary overlap, until finally the pianist takes over the recitative in the minor mode. The ending is most eloquent and moving:

Ex. 18

It can hardly be doubted that the composer had in mind Bach's
St John Passion, and particularly the aria 'Es ist vollbracht' with the
viol da gamba obbligato, and perhaps also the following chorus
on the chorale 'Jesu Leiden, Pein und Tot' with its accompanying
meditation for bass soloist. Mendelssohn's *adagio* may, in its turn,
have inspired César Franck, whose *Prélude, Chorale et Fugue* for solo
piano imitates so closely Mendelssohn's technique of spread
harmonies and his interweaving of chorale and reflective passages.
Czerny made an easy piano transcription of Mendelssohn's movement under the title of *Le Cygne mourant – Song of the dying swan*
with a heavily romantic excerpt from Czerny's diary describing a
scene imagined the morning after a hearing of the Sonata.

The finale, *molto allegro e vivace,* opens dramatically, being linked
to the chorale movement by a diminished seventh and creating
tension by deferring for some time any direct statement of the
tonic chord. The principal theme is a close relative of that of the
finale of the D minor Piano Concerto; its development poses the
question that is apt to arise with Mendelssohn's finales, whether
the material is not being over-stretched. An impression of super-
ficiality is increased by the salon style of keyboard figuration,
though the movement gains in solid musical interest as it continues.
One feels that Mendelssohn's improvisations at the piano must
often have sounded like this.

The Trios and the Second String Quintet

As early as 1832, when Mendelssohn was in Paris, he was thinking
of writing more concerted works in which the piano had a share.
On 21 January of that year he wrote to his sister Fanny: 'I should
like to compose a couple of good trios', and an early trio for
violin, viola and piano, listed by Grove among the unpublished
works, remains one of the tantalising will-o'-the-wisps of
Mendelssohn research. Not until 1839 did the first of the published
trios, in D minor, Op. 49, materialise. Schumann welcomed it
ecstatically in a *Neue Zeitschrift* article, hailing it as 'the master-Trio
of the age, as were the B flat and D major Trios of Beethoven and the
E flat Trio of Schubert in their time'. History has shown that
Schumann made no mistake; Mendelssohn's are the only important works of their kind between the composers Schumann named

and Brahms, although the piano trio was more intensively cultivated as an ensemble at that period than at any other. Schumann realised that the Mendelssohn trios were outstanding because, while not beyond the reach of good amateurs, their musical content and technical soundness satisfy the artist. The combination of violin, cello and piano no longer attracts composers, perhaps because it has never recovered from its associations with tea shops, hotel lounges and cinemas in the earlier years of the present century, but beside the relatively few great trios from Beethoven to Ravel there will always be a place of honour for Mendelssohn's.

The Trio in D minor combines with the composer's usual fluency a seriousness of intention that seems to go with his choice of this particular key; one thinks, for example, of the *Variations sérieuses* for piano, the sixth Organ Sonata, and the solemn opening of *Elijah*. The work is rich in warm, Italianate melodies that can be relished in turn by all three instruments, and though voices are sometimes raised against the squareness and phrase-repetitions of the first movement, it is put together with such skill and made to sound so well that its more naive features can be accepted by all but the hypercritical. There are also some structural features of uncommon interest. For example, the relative major key of F hardly makes an appearance in the first movement, while the principal theme is provided with ingenious counter-melodies at each repetition; one of these, a running counterpoint in semiquavers for violin and cello in octaves, plays a prominent part in the coda. The motive D – C sharp – D of the principal theme pervades the whole movement in various forms (sometimes diminished to a quaver group) in a way that seems prophetic of Brahms's use of the identical notes in his D major Symphony. Fifteen years had gone by since Mendelssohn wrote his early piano quartets, and although the keyboard writing is more dazzling than ever it no longer dominates the strings; each instrument is allowed to keep to its own technique and the balance of interest, as Schumann pointed out approvingly, is always held equally among the three partners. The piano part is often of concerto-like brilliancy; it was revised, apparently, at the instigation of Ferdinand Hiller, who urged the composer to make it a vehicle for his own performance in public by working into it some of the contemporary keyboard idioms developed by Chopin and Liszt.

In the *andante con moto tranquillo* we are reminded yet again of the better pieces in the *Songs without Words,* the resemblance being all the closer since the piano takes the lead in introducing themes. There is a middle section in the tonic minor, with Mendelssohn's favourite triplet accompaniment, after which the return of the principal theme is provided with refreshing new counter-melodies. The scherzo, marked *leggiero e vivace,* takes its cue from the playful keyboard opening in 6/8 time, with much use of the wrist and finger staccato for which Mendelssohn's playing was famous. The movement gains in vitality from the development of a motive of two semiquavers and a quaver, which results in displaced accents; the composer may have unwittingly borrowed this idea from the finale of Beethoven's little Piano Sonata in G, Op. 14, no. 2. The finale, *allegro assai appassionato,* is a rondo with a strongly characterised, almost Schubertian, main theme. The similarity to Schubert indeed goes further than this, being suggested by the opposition of the tonic key (D minor) to the submediant B flat and thence to Neapolitan harmony based on the flattened supertonic (E flat). In this movement also the piano is generally the initiator of new ideas, including a theme in the long-deferred F major which is a derivative of the principal theme. An exception, however, is the cantabile tune which suddenly appears in the submediant key of B flat in the middle of the movement; this is obviously conceived in terms of the violin and cello, and the piano takes a subordinate role in presenting it. The same melody turns up again in the coda, again in B flat, but a determined modulation to D major allows it to be heard in that key (with the unusual marking *f e dolce*). The major key is maintained, with references to the principal theme, and the Trio is brought to an end with a page of pure display.

The C minor Trio, Op. 60, written six years later and dedicated to Spohr, is in some ways finer than its companion. It differs in seeming to be conceived entirely in instrumental terms, whereas the earlier Trio is replete with cantabile melodies and owes much to the romantic *Lied.* In the C minor Trio the urgency of the opening, over a pedal C sustained by the cello, produces an impression of controlled tension and of spaciousness which discloses an unfamiliar aspect of the composer's personality:

Ex. 19

This sense of drama is maintained as the instruments exchange roles and develop the theme jointly for a few bars that are again prophetic of Brahms in their sweeping arpeggios for the strings and powerful chords on the piano. The instruments then divide their presentation of a sequel to the opening, violin and cello sharing the melody, while the piano accompanies with figuration derived, by diminution and inversion, from the theme itself. A great deal of use is made of these derived figures, which continue as accompaniment to the suave main theme of the second subject, in E flat major. The working-out of these three pieces of thematic material is admirable in its inventiveness and rhythmic impetus; Mendelssohn never wrote a stronger sonata-form movement. Especially worthy of note are the variations made in the character of the principal theme by substituting staccato keyboard touch, or mixed detached and slurred bowings, for the long slurs of its original presentation. At certain climactic points the main theme is mirrored between violin and cello, and in the coda those instruments play an augmented version of the theme against its original version on the piano. Canonic imitation, always one of Mendelssohn's readiest devices, is used here with effective reserve. In general, the movement derives much of its powerful sonority from the exploitation of all three instruments over their whole compass and from the use of combined arpeggios by contrary motion. The key-system is beautifully proportioned, and the very occasional employment of enharmonic modulation is all the more telling because of its comparative rarity in Mendelssohn's harmonic style. The coda is imposing in dimensions and contains some particularly happy modulations to the flat side of the main key, and a fiery conclusion with octave passages for the piano.

The gentle sentiment of the *andante espressivo* has a specially appealing character, due largely to the pervasive repetitions of its first four notes. In the central section Mendelssohn makes a key-change parallel to the one in the corresponding movement of the D minor Trio: in this case, the modulation is to the tonic minor, E flat. The scherzo belongs to the duple-time, toccata-like type with a great deal of fugato texture. It has a distinct Hungarian-gipsy flavour, which becomes stronger in the middle section, with its fluctuations between major and minor and its trills and 'Scotch snaps' on the first quaver of the bar. Every detail of this complex but economically ordered movement deserves the closest attention. On its return, the main theme of the scherzo is shortened and altered to allow the 'gipsy' motive to be embodied in a coda where the sound is gradually attenuated almost to vanishing point.

The finale begins in rather an arch manner, with a jog-trot theme characterised by the interval of the ninth on the upbeat of the phrase. This theme is not unlike that of Schumann's piano piece *Aufschwung*, Op. 12, no. 2. Greater seriousness of intent is revealed in the continuation of the movement, reaching its climax in what is for Mendelssohn always a gesture of spiritual devotion – the introduction of a chorale-like melody, though the identification of this as the Lutheran chorale 'Gelobet seist du' seems doubtful. The return of this theme, in C major, is the emotional peak of the movement and of the entire work; it can hardly be denied, however, that at this point the medium of the piano trio is over-strained by quasi-orchestral treatment and that a sense of bombast mars the ending, with its attempt to round off the Trio by linking the chorale with the light-weight principal theme.

The year 1845 also saw the completion of the second Quintet for strings, in B flat, Op. 87. The reputation of this seldom-played work has risen and fallen with the passage of time. We have seen that the English writer Chorley, writing within ten years of its publication, thought it greatly superior to the Quartet in A minor (see p. 32). Sir George Grove, too, pronounced it a splendid work. The modern view is more in line with that of Wilhelm Altmann, who in *Cobbett's Cyclopaedic Survey of Chamber Music* expresses his opinion that the middle movements are better than the outer ones.

The first movement, despite much superficial activity and the composer's unfailing dexterity in modulating, seems to lack real vitality and freshness. Even its opening, an arpeggio first violin theme over tremolando chords, does little more than retrace what had already been done in the D major Quartet, Op. 44, no. 1, while what follows is less interesting than the sequel in the earlier work. Attention is often focused on the first violin, which is given concerto-like figuration.

With the *andante scherzando* the temperature of inspiration rises noticeably. This belongs to the less rapid and less brilliant type of Mendelssohnian scherzo. It is beautifully composed and scored, and has interesting rhythmic features: the note-groupings often have the effect of displacing the accents, especially when bowed across bar-lines, and syncopations are freely used. Contrasts of arco and pizzicato and variety of bowings enhance the subtlety of phrase-articulation. The texture is linear almost throughout, but harmonically there are impressive moments, like the interplay between F major and G minor occurring near the end.

The other outstanding movement of this Quintet, the *adagio e lento*, can be described as a rhapsody on an elegiac theme announced in the opening bars, and having some resemblance to the 'processional' movement of the Italian Symphony. The first violin almost takes on the personality of a coloratura soprano, while the accompaniments are dramatic, full of shuddering chords, tremolandos, and violent dynamics. Harmonic and instrumental colours are of unusual intensity: an example of the former is the progression of the violins in the fifth bar, and of the latter in the passage where the cello soars far above the rest of the ensemble.

The finale, following without a break, is rather an empty movement, in spite of attempts to animate it with busy semiquaver figures and syncopated ryhthms. Nor is there a strong feeling for the medium. The effect is that of an orchestra with depleted forces rather than the lucid chamber texture the composer had so often handled with sensitive judgment.

The Last Quartets

Mendelssohn's ten years of married life had brought him much contentment and a refuge from the increasing stresses of his public career. But his ties with his two sisters, and especially the elder one who had shared in his musical upbringing, remained as close as ever, and he suffered a collapse on hearing the news of Fanny's death on 17 May 1847. In the hope of hastening his recovery from the shock he was persuaded to spend the summer in Switzerland with his wife and a few friends, and while at Interlaken he composed his last completed chamber music work, the String Quartet in F minor (Op. 80), in memory of his sister. The poignant circumstances of its composition, but even more the character of the work itself, give it a special place in the composer's legacy. Some have thought that it might have been the beginning of a new phase in Mendelssohn's artistic development, combining the independent vigour of his earlier years with the poise and polish of his maturity. It contains some of his finest musical thought, profound, passionate, and vitally rhythmic.

At its heart stands the slow movement, for which the model may well have been the *adagio molto e mesto* of Beethoven's Op. 59, no. 1. But it may also hold closer personal associations. On 14 June 1830 Mendelssohn had enclosed in a letter to Fanny a miniature piano piece he had written for her, with an inconclusive ending like that of the ritornello of Schumann's song 'Im wunderschönen Monat Mai'. The *adagio* of the Quartet may remind us of Beethoven; it may also recall the intermezzo added to the Quintet in A in memory of Rietz; but most of all, perhaps, it resembles a mournful transformation of that private 'Song without Words':

Ex. 20
(a)

'Lied', 1830

Andante [closing bars]

dim.

pp

Quartet Op. 80, 1847
(b)

Adagio

p

p

The first movement to the Quartet also arouses memories of Beethoven – in this the parallel being with a Beethoven Quartet in the same key, Op. 95:

Ex. 21

The resemblance, admittedly, is short-lived; Beethoven's characteristically forceful theme, like Mendelssohn's, turns within a confined space, but is terse and abrupt, whereas Mendelssohn extends his opening into an eight-bar period. This is only the first limb of the principal subject, however; the theme quoted is followed by others, two of which represent the more aggressive and the gentler aspects of the same idea:

Ex. 22

The material of the second subject group leads to surprising harmonic progressions that suggest an advance towards the harmonic revolution that was about to take place elsewhere, even though Wagner at this time had got no further than *Lohengrin*:

Ex. 23

The development is mainly concerned with Ex. 22 (*a*), which thereafter plays a comparatively minor role in the recapitulation and coda. Its rhythmic pattern, however, is a feature of the return of the principal theme, with the first violin surveying the process from an extreme altitude. The coda, more than any other part of the Quartet, approaches Beethoven's concentrated intensity, both in the final working of the first-subject themes and in the extended *presto* coda.

For the second movement Mendelssohn seems to renounce all his customary varieties of scherzo; instead, he follows Beethoven's transformation of the old minuet into a bizarre, almost savage, triple-time dance. Syncopated rhythms, harsh dissonances both prepared and unprepared, a bass that either forces its way upwards by chromatic semitones or remains firmly static, octave passages, and phrases separated off by rests, all contribute to the sense of disquiet. The trio section, too, is extraordinary. Viola and cello introduce in octaves a passacaglia-like theme, above which the violins enter in sixths with a kind of macabre waltz. The writing remains in three parts throughout – a trio in the literal sense. Here it is not so much Beethoven who comes to mind as Mahler; ironically it was a performance of one of Mendelssohn's weaker works, *St Paul*, that helped to establish Mahler as a conductor.

A relationship between the *adagio* and Beethoven's Op. 59, no. 1, has been sugggested. Did Mendelssohn learn from his friend Nottebohm that Beethoven had written beside his sketch of the opening of his *adagio molto e mesto*: 'Eine Trauer-weide oder Akazien-Baum aufs Grab meines Bruders' ('A weeping willow or acacia-tree on my brother's grave') and borrow this as the unspoken text of his own lamentation? The score is full of dynamic markings, as if to emphasise every nuance of feeling. Beginning with a gentle flow and with smooth harmonies, the movement gradually becomes more troubled, with harsher dissonances and broken, sobbing rhythms. At the climax the remote keys of E major and minor are reached and quitted enharmonically – a procedure which, as we have seen before, is relatively uncommon with Mendelssohn.

The finale is a tempestuous mingling of sorrow and despair expressed through contrasting themes, the first restlessly syncopated, the second full of drooping cadences. But there are also moments when the music becomes almost athematic, with writing of a strange bareness found nowhere else in Mendelssohn. How many, without knowing the source and context, would recognise as his such an impressionistic passage as the following?

Ex. 24

The recapitulation of the principal theme is accompanied by a new feature, a counterpoint in triplet quavers added by the first violin above the syncopations of the theme, producing a polyrhythmic effect. Although by this time the experiments of the earlier 'cyclic' works had been abandoned, it may not be too far-fetched to identify the triplet figures with those that play so extensive a part in the first movement. Mendelssohn had used, and even abused, the tarantella and saltarello rhythms many times before. But in this context they no longer express carefree high spirits, but rather accentuate the mood of despair in which this tragic work ends. The autograph of the F minor Quartet is dated September 1847. Less than two months later, on 4 November, the composer himself died. It is touching to read what Julius Benedict, who had looked over the shoulder of the twelve-year-old Mendelssohn as he wrote out his first published chamber work, had to say about this last Quartet:

It would be difficult to cite any piece of music which so completely impresses the listener with a sensation of gloomy foreboding, of anguish of mind, and of the most poetic melancholy, as does this masterly and eloquent composition.

One reason for believing that Mendelssohn, had he lived longer, might have occupied himself more intensively with chamber music is that we have part of yet another string quartet dating from these last months. The miscellany published posthumously as Op. 81 affords another example of the inscrutable ways of the composer's executors. The four pieces it comprises represent various periods and styles, and in no way constitute a coherent work. The E flat Fugue has already been noticed: it is not much more than an academic exercise dating from 1827, and scored for string quartet like other exercises of similar type still in manuscript. The string writing is unidiomatic, though there are some interesting experiments in spacing: in places there is a gap of nearly three octaves between the middle instruments. The Capriccio in E minor belongs to the year 1843, a period when Mendelssohn seems otherwise to have produced little chamber music. Its key, and a certain exuberance in the first violin part, link it stylistically with the Violin Concerto of the following year. In structure it resembles the piano *Preludes and Fugues*; an amiable 12/8 introduction ending in a short violin cadenza leads to a monumentally large and elaborate fugato. The subject is made up of two contrasting motives, each extended sequentially, and these two ideas, together with two counter-themes of arpeggio formation, make up most of the material. The two halves of the subject are worked together, and later both they and the arpeggio counter-themes are inverted and redeveloped in that form. This is genuine string polyphony, increasing in interest as it progresses, and is worth more than the occasional token performance.

The other two pieces are thought to be the middle movements of a quartet whose other movements were either never written or were destroyed by the composer. The first is an *andante* in E major, the second a scherzo in A minor. One may conjecture that the first movement and the finale would have been in E minor, a key Mendelssohn always favoured for serious purposes. If this were the case, might he have intended the Capriccio of 1843 to stand as the finale, if only since he lacked energy and time to write something fresh? The Capriccio would then occupy its appropriate place in Op. 81. One might even postulate a three-movement Quartet starting in E major and finishing, like the Italian Symphony, in the minor mode.

The E major movement is a set of variations on an original theme twenty bars in length. In the first variation, the melody is taken over by the viola, with a light accompaniment for violins and an occasional pizzicato cello note. In the second (*un poco più animato*) it is freely worked in triplet quavers, and in the two following linked variations it is still more freely paraphrased by first violin and cello. This leads by way of a brief violin cadenza to a final *presto* variation in 6/8 time. Another short cadenza leads back to the theme, which is not, however, repeated in its entirety but turns into a coda resembling the first variation, with the viola again to the fore. The final chord of E major is evidently meant to point both backwards and forwards: as the dominant of A minor it heralds the scherzo, the last movement of this kind Mendelssohn was ever to write, and one of his best.

The particular charm of this example lies in its rhythmic organisation. Ostensibly it moves regularly in 6/8 time with four-bar phrases, but in practice such metrical performance would make nonsense of the music. A twentieth-century composer would almost certainly have barred the opening as 9/8 – 12/8 – 3/8 – 9/8 and so on, following the harmonic rhythm and the recurrence of similar groupings. The variable rhythmic units, which the performers must discover for themselves, give the piece a remarkable plasticity. In addition, various means are used to create an effect of constantly changing densities, like the atmosphere in hill country; at one moment, the number of notes in a chord or contrapuntal passage may be as great as five or six, at another it is reduced to a single thread. Dialoguing, scales by contrary motion, the reinforcement of the principal theme in parallel thirds, are among the devices employed. As the movement nears its end, the swirling figuration seems to crystallise into homophonic chords played with the lightest of bows up to the final pizzicato cadence. The pure poetry of this scherzo equals anything Mendelssohn had achieved in his young days; that he should at the last have regained his facility should be a cause of gratitude, though it underlines the tragedy of a creative life brought to an untimely end.

It was in Paris that Mendelssohn's chamber music was first appreciated at its true worth, and it is understandable that the clarity, logic, restraint and finish of his work should ever since have made a particular appeal to the French mind. His musical personality had never been better summed up than in the words of Camille Bellaigue, who published his life of Mendelssohn in 1907, sixty years after the composer's death:

Lui-même, le musicien allemand, où donc, en le quittant, allons-nous le placer, le laisser pour jamais? Dans la région des idées claires et fines, des sentiments comme des sensations délicates et des passions tempérées. Il a dit rarement des choses sublimes; parfois il en a dit de hautes, de nobles, et très souvent d'exquises. Mais parce qu'il n'en a jamais dit d'obscures, encore moins d'inintelligibles, on affecte de le dédaigner aujourd'hui.

Contempt, indifference, and – over a large part of Europe in the middle years of this century – racial and cultural ostracism have in turn been Mendelssohn's lot since Bellaigue wrote those words. By one of history's ironies, the last and most hostile phase has actually helped to bring about a revaluation of his work; for a whole generation of German musicians had grown up with little or no acquaintance with it, and after the restoration of freedom and sanity of thought was therefore able to listen to it with fresh and unprejudiced minds. Elsewhere in the world, harmful and irrelevant social and religious associations have been allowed to fall away from the composer's image, revealing the best of his work, including the chamber music, as a unique and indispensable part of our heritage of nineteenth-century culture.

Additional note on the Octet in E Flat, *Op. 20*

A facsimile of the holograph score of the Octet, formerly owned by Eduard Rietz and now in the collection of the Gertrude Clarke Whittall Foundation in the Library of Congress, is in course of publication by Vienna House Inc., New York. The facsimile, which is to include a critical introduction, will be produced under the editorial supervision of Jon Newsom, of the Music Division of Library of Congress. The holograph score reveals some important differences between what is presumed to be Mendelssohn's original version and the parts and score published in 1832 and 1848 respectively.